TOTAL
READING

AMERICAN
EDUCATION
PUBLISHING™

Columbus, Ohio

Copyright © 2005 School Specialty Publishing. Published by American Education Publishing™, an imprint of School Specialty Publishing, a member of the School Specialty Family.

Send all inquiries to:
School Specialty Publishing
8720 Orion Place
Columbus, OH 43240-2111

ISBN 0-7696-3881-3

6 7 8 9 10 WAL 09 08 07 06

Table of Contents

Letters and Sounds

Reading Comprehension

Name _____

Writing the Alphabet

Directions: Trace the alphabet. Use the numbers on the arrows as you trace.

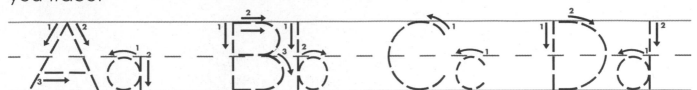

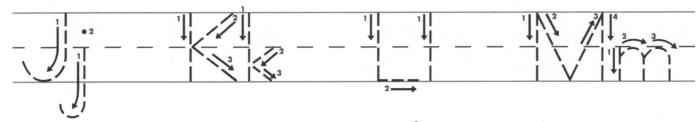

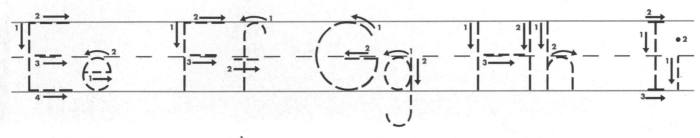

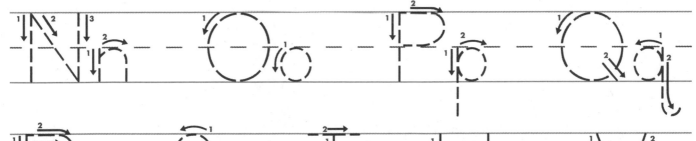

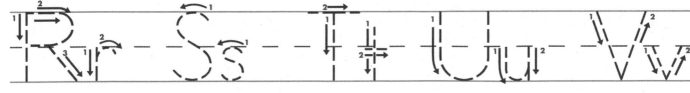

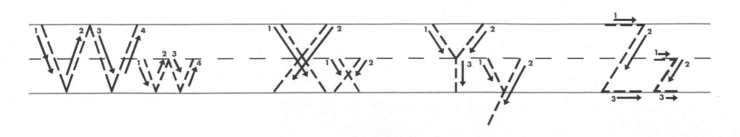

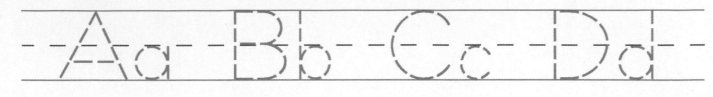

Name _____

Writing the Alphabet

Directions: Trace the letters **Aa-Mm**. Then, practice writing them on the lines below.

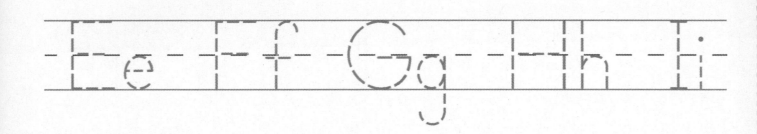

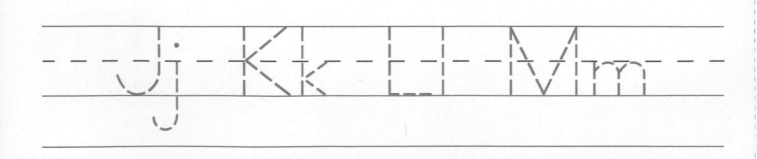

Name _____

Writing the Alphabet

Directions: Trace the letters **Nn-Zz**. Then, practice writing them on the lines below.

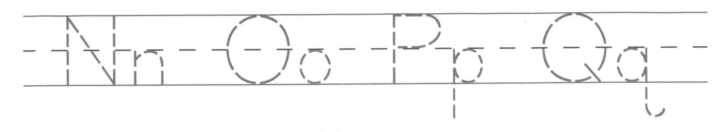

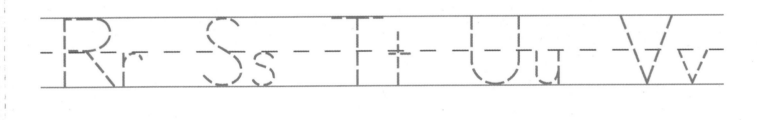

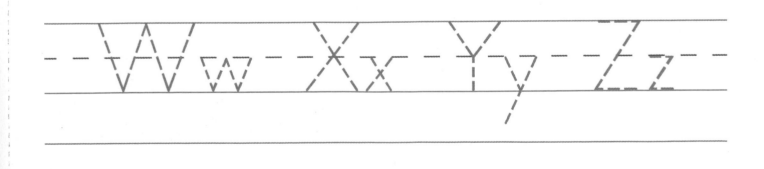

7

Name _____

Write and Hear Mm

M and **m** are letter partners.

Map begins with the sound of **Mm**.

Directions: Trace the letter. Write it on the line.

M _ _ _ _ _ _ _ _ _ _ _ _ _ _ _ _ _

m _ _ _ _ _ _ _ _ _ _ _ _ _ _ _ _ _

Directions: Color the pictures whose names begin with the sound of **m**.

Write and Hear Ss

S and **s** are letter partners.

Sock begins with the sound of **Ss**.

Directions: Trace the letter. Write it on the line.

S - - - - - - - - - - - - - - - - - -

_____

s - - - - - - - - - - - - - - - - - -

Directions: Circle the socks with pictures whose names begin with the sound of **s**.

Name _____

Write and Hear Tt

T and **t** are letter partners.

Tiger begins with the sound of **Tt**.

Directions: Trace the letter. Write it on the line.

Directions: Color the pictures whose names begin with the sound of **t**.

Name _____

Write and Hear Hh

H and **h** are letter partners.

Hat begins with the sound of **Hh**.

Directions: Trace the letter. Write it on the line.

H -

h -

Directions: Play Tic-Tac-Toe. Find three pictures in a row whose names begin with the sound of **h**. Draw a line through them.

Name _____

Write and Hear Kk

K and **k** are letter partners.

Kitten begins with the sound of **Kk**.

Directions: Trace the letter. Write it on the line.

K - - - - - - - - - - - - - - - - - - -

k - - - - - - - - - - - - - - - - - - -

Directions: Color the pictures whose names begin with the sound of **k**.

  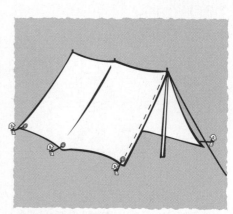

Name _____

Write and Hear Bb

B and **b** are letter partners.

Ball begins with the sound of **Bb**.

Directions: Trace the letter. Write it on the line.

B -

b -

Directions: Color the bow if the name of the picture on the box begins with the sound of **b**.

Name _____

Write and Hear Ff

F and **f** are letter partners.

Fox begins with the sound of **Ff**.

Directions: Trace the letter. Write it on the line.

F –

f –

Directions: Help the farmer find the fox. Draw a line through the pictures whose names begin with the sound of **f**.

Name _____

Write and Hear Gg

G and **g** are letter partners.

Goat begins with the sound of **Gg**.

Directions: Trace the letter. Write it on the line.

G -

g -

Directions: Write **g** if the name of the picture begins with the sound of **g**.

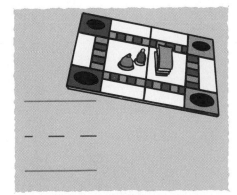

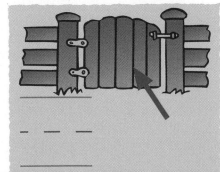

Name _____

Write and Hear Ll

L and I are letter partners.

Leaf begins with the sound of Ll.

Directions: Trace the letter. Write it on the line.

L

L

Directions: Color the leaves with pictures whose names begin with the sound of I.

Write and Hear Nn

N and **n** are letter partners.

Nest begins with the sound of **Nn**.

Directions: Trace the letter. Write it on the line.

N -

n -

Directions: Color the pictures whose names begin with the sound of **n**.

Name _____

Write and Hear Dd

D and **d** are letter partners.

Desk begins with the sound of **Dd**.

Directions: Trace the letter. Write it on the line.

D -

d -

Directions: Color the pictures whose names begin with the sound of **d**.

Name _____

Write and Hear Ww

W and **w** are letter partners.

Window begins with the sound of **Ww**.

Directions: Trace the letter. Write it on the line.

W -

W -

Directions: Color the curtains if the name of the picture begins with the sound of **w**.

Name _____

Write and Hear Cc

C and **c** are letter partners.

Cap begins with the sound of **Cc**.

Directions: Trace the letter. Write it on the line.

C -

c -

Directions: Play Tic-Tac-Toe. Find three pictures in a row whose names begin with the sound of **c**. Draw a line through them.

Name _____

Write and Hear Jj

J and **j** are letter partners.

Jacket begins with the sound of **Jj**.

Directions: Trace the letter. Write it on the line.

J

j

Directions: Color the jack-in-the-box if the name of its picture begins with the sound of **j**.

Name _____

Write and Hear Rr

R and **r** are letter partners.

Ring begins with the sound of **Rr**.

Directions: Trace the letter. Write it on the line.

R – – – – – – – – – – – – – – – – –

r – – – – – – – – – – – – – – – – –

Directions: Write **r** on the line if the name of the picture begins with the sound of **r**.

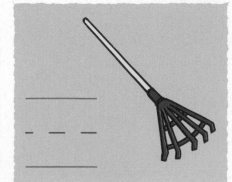

22

Consonant Sounds

Name _____

Write and Hear Pp

P and **p** are letter partners.

Pen begins with the sound of **Pp**.

Directions: Trace the letter. Write it on the line.

P -

p -

Directions: Color the pictures whose names begin with the sound of **p**.

Name _____

Write and Hear Vv

V and **v** are letter partners.

Vase begins with the sound of **Vv**.

Directions: Trace the letter. Write it on the line.

V ─ ─ ─ ─ ─ ─ ─ ─ ─ ─ ─ ─ ─ ─ ─ ─ ─ ─

v ─ ─ ─ ─ ─ ─ ─ ─ ─ ─ ─ ─ ─ ─ ─ ─ ─ ─

Directions: Trace the vases with pictures whose names begin with the sound of **v**. Use a crayon.

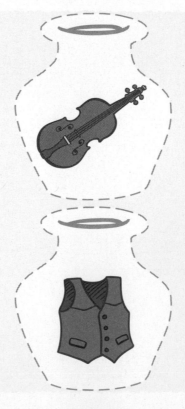

Name _____

Write and Hear Yy

Y and **y** are letter partners.

Yellow begins with the sound of **Yy**.

Directions: Trace the letter. Write it on the line.

Directions: Play Tic-Tac-Toe. Find three pictures in a row whose names begin with the sound of **y**. Draw a line through them.

Name _____

Write and Hear Zz

Z and **z** are letter partners.

Zero begins with the sound of **Zz**.

Directions: Trace the letter. Write it on the line.

Z

Z

Directions: Help the zebra find the zoo. Connect all the pictures whose names begin with the sound of **z** from the zebra to the zoo.

Name _____

Write and Hear Qq

Q and **q** are letter partners.

Queen begins with the sound of **Qq**.

Directions: Trace the letter. Write it on the line.

Q

q

Directions: Write **q** on the line if the name in the picture begins with the sound of **q**.

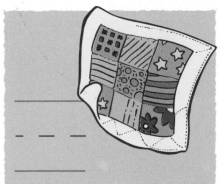

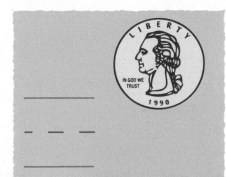

Name _____

Write and Hear Xx

X and **x** are letter partners.

Box ends with the sound of **Xx**.

Directions: Trace the letter. Write it on the line.

box

X _

X _

Directions: Look at the letter at the end of the row. Then, color the pictures whose names end with the sound of that letter. Circle the pictures whose names **end** with **x**.

Name _____

Beginning Consonants: Bb, Cc, Dd, Ff

Beginning consonants are the sounds that come at the beginning of words. Consonants are the letters **b**, **c**, **d**, **f**, **g**, **h**, **j k**, **l**, **m**, **n**, **p**, **q**, **r**, **s**, **t**, **v**, **w**, **x**, **y**, and **z**.

Directions: Say the name of each letter. Say the sound each letter makes. Circle the letters that make the beginning sound for each picture.

Bb   Cc   Dd   Ff

Bb Dd   Ff Cc   Cc Dd   Ff Bb

Bb Dd   Ff Cc   Cc Dd   Ff Bb

Name _____

Beginning Consonants: Bb, Cc, Dd, Ff

Directions: Say the name of each letter. Say the sound each letter makes. Draw a line from each letter to the picture which begins with that sound.

Ff

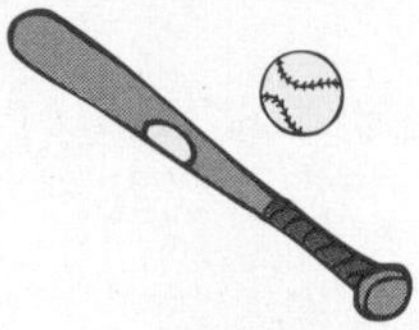

Dd

Cc

Bb

Dd

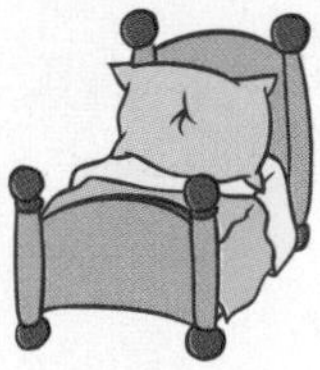

Ff

Cc

Bb

Name _____

Beginning Consonants: Gg, Hh, Jj, Kk

Directions: Say the name of each letter. Say the sound each letter makes. Trace the letter pair that makes the beginning sound in each picture.

| Gg | Hh | Jj | Kk |

Kk   Hh

Gg   Kk

Gg   Hh

Jj   Gg

Name _____

Beginning Consonants: Gg, Hh, Jj, Kk

Directions: Say the name of each letter. Say the sound each letter makes. Draw a line from each letter pair to the picture which begins with that sound.

Gg

Kk

Hh

Jj

Kk

Hh

Jj

Gg

Name _____

Beginning Consonants: Ll, Mm, Nn, Pp

Directions: Say the name of each letter. Say the sound each letter makes. Trace the letters. Then, draw a line from each letter pair to the picture which begins with that sound.

| Ll | Mm | Nn | Pp |

Ll

Mm

Nn

Pp

Beginning Consonants: Ll, Mm, Nn, Pp

Directions: Say the name of each letter. Say the sound each letter makes. Trace the letter pair that makes the beginning sound in each picture.

 Ll  Mm  Nn  Pp

Mm Ll

Mm Pp

Ll Nn

Pp Mm

Beginning Consonants: Qq, Rr, Ss, Tt

Directions: Say the name of each letter. Say the sound each letter makes. Trace the letter pair in the boxes. Then, color the picture which begins with that sound.

Qq   Rr   Ss   Tt

Tt

Qq

Rr

Ss

Name _____

Beginning Consonants: Qq, Rr, Ss, Tt

Directions: Say the name of each letter. Say the sound each letter makes. Draw a line from each letter pair to the picture which begins with that sound.

Qq

Ss

Rr

Tt

Tt

Ss

Rr

Qq

Beginning Consonants: Vv, Ww, Xx, Yy, Zz

Directions: Say the name of each letter. Say the sound each letter makes. Trace the letters. Then, draw a line from each letter pair to the picture which begins with that sound.

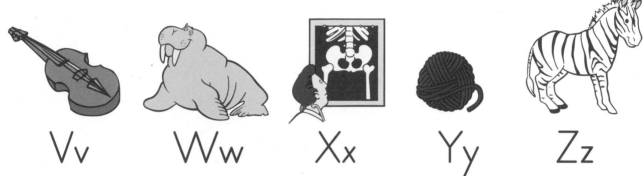

Vv   Ww   Xx   Yy   Zz

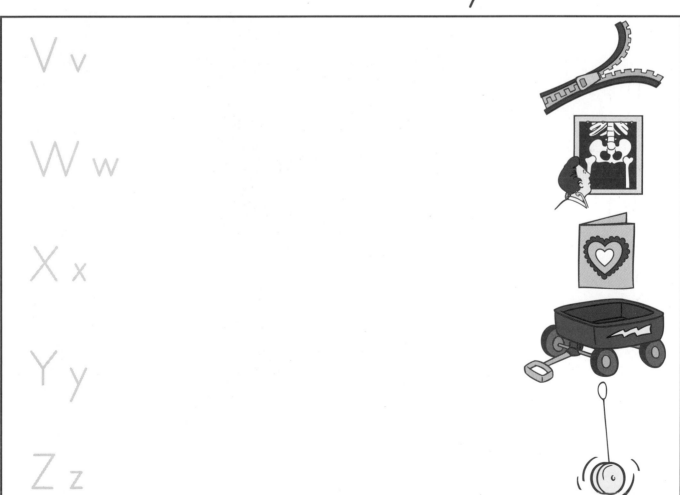

V v

W w

X x

Y y

Z z

Name _____

Beginning Consonants: Vv, Ww, Xx, Yy, Zz

Directions: Say the name of each letter. Say the sound each letter makes. Then, draw a line from each letter pair to the picture which begins with that sound.

Vv

Zz

Xx

Yy

Ww

Vv

Zz

Yy

Ww

Xx

38

Name _____

Match Letters and Sounds

Directions: Cut out each letter at the bottom of the page. Find the picture whose name begins with the sound of that letter. Glue the letter in the box beside the picture.

z d t w c r

Name _____

How Do I Begin?

Directions: Say the name of each picture. Write the beginning sound for each picture.

 _____ at

 _____ oat

 _____ ite

 _____ am

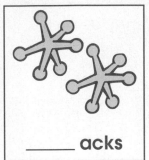 _____ acks

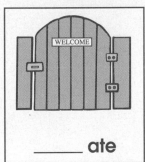 _____ ate

 _____ ey

 _____ appy

Directions: Write each word next to its beginning sound.

g _ _ _ _ _ _ _ _ _

g _ _ _ _ _ _ _ _ _

h _ _ _ _ _ _ _ _ _

h _ _ _ _ _ _ _ _ _

j _ _ _ _ _ _ _ _ _

j _ _ _ _ _ _ _ _ _

k _ _ _ _ _ _ _ _ _

k _ _ _ _ _ _ _ _ _

Name _____

How Do I Begin Again?

Directions: Say each letter sound. Color the pictures in each row that begin with that sound.

 b

 c

 d

f

Directions: Say the name of each picture. Write the beginning sound for each picture.

  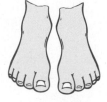 

_____ed _____og _____eet _____up

Name _____

Review: Beginning Consonants

Directions: Say each picture name. Circle the letter that stands for the beginning sound.

p m n

v t s

f g p

s c p

m g v

g p n

m p n

t g p

s l c

g l c

p b f

v l t

Name _____

Review: Beginning Consonants

Directions: Look at the letters in the boxes. Then, say each picture name. Draw a line from the letter to the picture whose name begins with that sound.

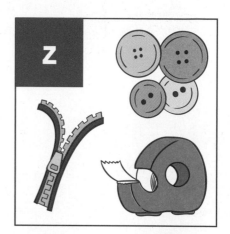

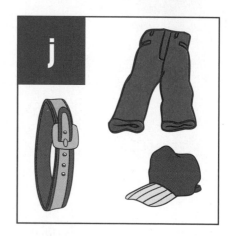

44

Consonant Sounds

Name _____

Review

Directions: Write the letter that makes the beginning sound for each picture.

___ ar

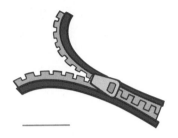

___ ipper

___ ite

___ etter

___ oat

___ ose

___ un

___ ouse

___ urtle

___ lasses

___ ar

___ og

How Does It End?

Ending consonants are the sounds that come at the end of words.

Directions: Write a letter from the box to complete each word.

m   k   b   n   p   r   l   d   g

dru __

sta __

be __

tai __

bi __

lo __

fa __

mo __

boo __

And Finally...

Directions: Say each picture name. Write the ending sound for each picture.

tu ___

pai ___

pa ___

lo ___

hoo ___

mu ___

boo ___

ha ___

shel ___

lea ___

cra ___

li ___

gir ___

bea ___

broo ___

Name _____

Ending Consonants: b, d, f

Directions: Say the name of each picture. Then, write the letter that makes the ending sound for each picture.

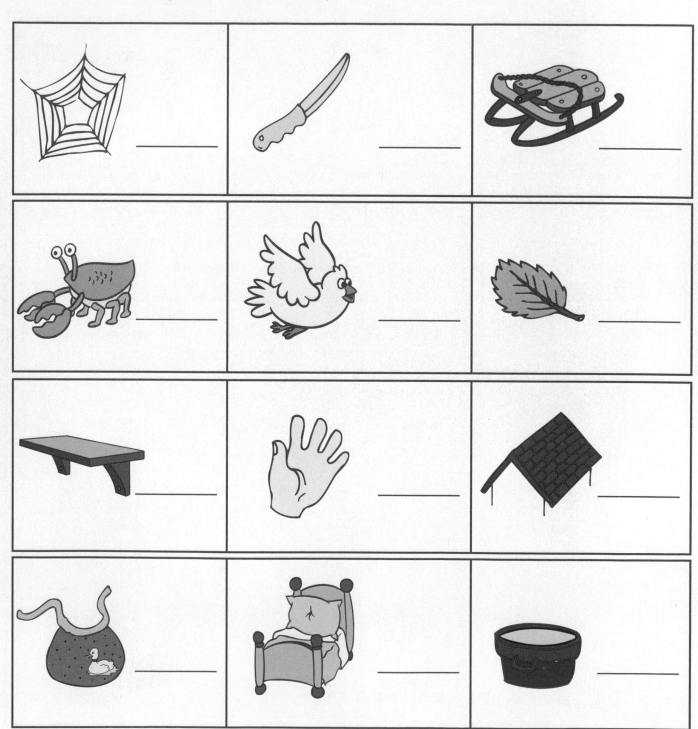

48

Consonant Sounds

Name _____

Ending Consonants: g, m, n

Directions: Say the name of each picture. Draw a line from each letter to the pictures which end with that sound.

g

m

n

g

m

n

Name _____

Ending Consonants: k, l, p

Directions: Trace the letters in each row. Say the name of each picture. Then, color the pictures in each row which end with that sound.

k
  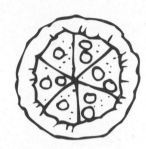 

l

p

Name _____

Ending Consonants: r, s, t, x

Directions: Say the name of each picture. Then, circle the ending sound for each picture.

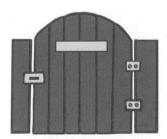 r s t x

 r s t x

 r s t x

 r s t x

 r s t x

 r s t x

 r s t x

 r s t x

Name _____

Consonant Review

Directions: One letter is missing in each word. Write the missing letter on the line.

_____ og

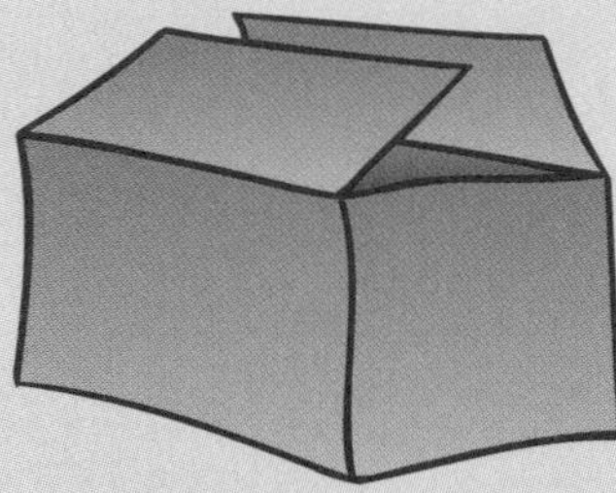

_____ bo_____

_____ un

_____ he_____

_____ tu_____ ip

_____ op

_____ to_____

_____ lea_____

wa_____ on

52

Name _____

Consonant Review

Directions: Write all the missing consonants.

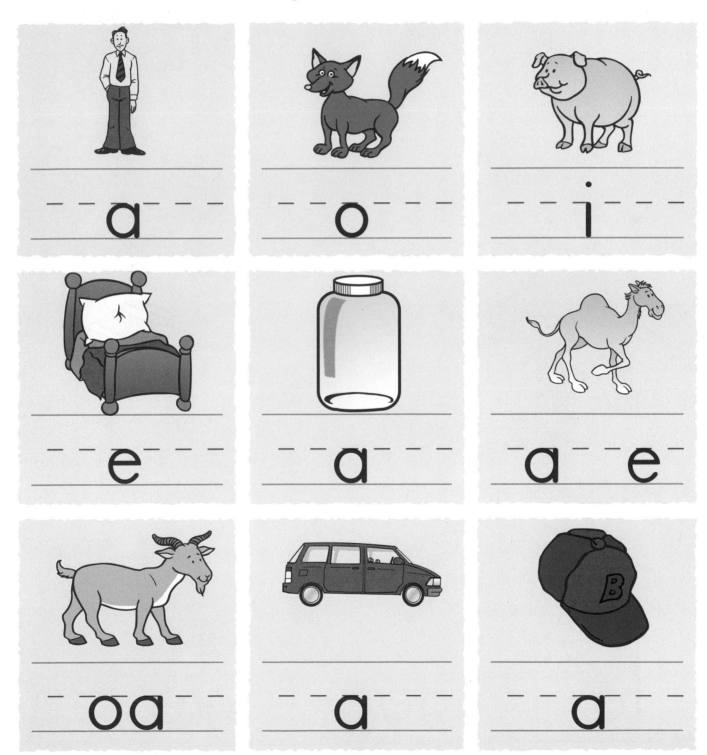

Name _____

Meet Short a

Listen for the sound of short **a** in **van**.

Directions: Trace the letter. Write it on the line.

 van

A

a

Directions: Color the pictures whose names have the short **a** sound.

Short a Maze

Directions: Help the cat get to the bag. Connect all the pictures whose names have the short **a** sound from the cat to the bag.

55

Name _____

Meet Short i

Listen for the sound of short **i** in **pig**.

Directions: Trace the letter. Write it on the line.

pig

I ─

i ─

Directions: Say the name of each picture. Color the trim on the bib if the name has the short **i** sound.

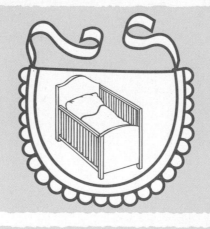

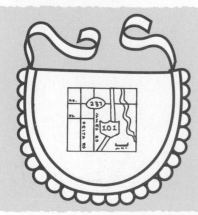

Name _____

Read and Color Short i

Directions: Say the name of each picture. Color the pictures whose names have the short **i** sound. The words in the box will give you hints.

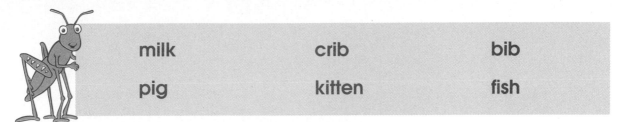

milk	crib	bib
pig	kitten	fish

Name _____

Meet Short u

Listen for the sound of short **u** in **bug**.

Directions: Trace the letter. Write it on the line.

bug

U — — — — — — — — — — — — — — — —

U — — — — — — — — — — — — — — — —

Directions: Say the name of each picture. Color the sun yellow if you hear the short **u** sound in the name.

Name _____

Short u Tic-Tac-Toe

Directions: Color the pictures whose names have the short **u** sound. Then, play Tic-Tac-Toe. Draw a line through three colored pictures in a row.

	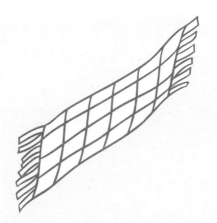	

Name _____

Meet Short o

Listen for the sound of short **o** in **fox**.

Directions: Trace the letter. Write it on the line.

fox

Directions: Say the name of each picture. Write **o** under the picture if the name has the short **o** sound.

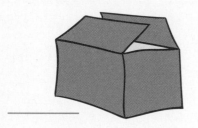

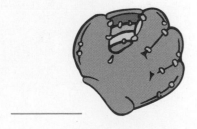

Name _____

Find Short o Words

Directions: Draw a line under each picture whose name has the short **o** sound.

Directions: The words that match the underlined pictures above are hidden in this puzzle. Circle the words. They may go **across** or **down**.

I T L J B Z

M O O C O T

O P G U X U

P D O G L P

Name _____

Meet Short e

Listen for the sound of short **e** in **hen**.

Directions: Trace the letter. Write it on the line.

h**en**

E

e

Directions: Color the pictures whose names have the short **e** sound.

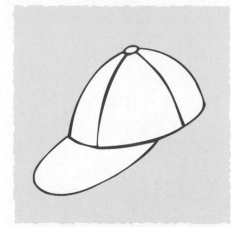

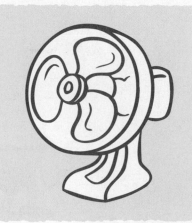
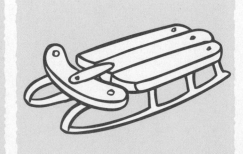

Name _____

A Matching Game

Directions: Draw a line to connect each picture with its matching short **e** word.

men

jet

hen

web

ten

bed

63

Meet Long a

Listen for the sound of long **a** in **cake**.

Directions: Color the pictures whose names have the long **a** sound.

cake

Name _____

Write Long a

The letters **a__e** usually stand for the long **a** sound.

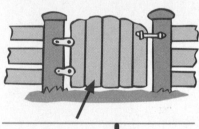

lake

Directions: Write the missing vowels.

c a v e   g   m   v   s

c   g   c   p   g   t

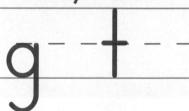

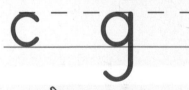

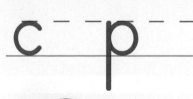

r   k   c   n   w   v

Name _____

Meet Long i

Listen for the sound of long **i** in **bike**. Look for **i__e**.

Directions: Fill in the circle beside the name of the picture.

b**i**k**e**

- ○ dim
- ○ date
- ○ dime

- ○ five
- ○ fix
- ○ fame

- ○ kite
- ○ cat
- ○ kit

- ○ pane
- ○ pin
- ○ pine

- ○ tin
- ○ tire
- ○ tale

- ○ red
- ○ ride
- ○ rid

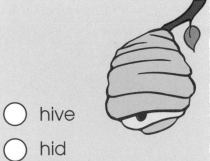
- ○ hive
- ○ hid
- ○ had

- ○ nip
- ○ name
- ○ nine

- ○ fame
- ○ fire
- ○ fin

Name _____

Meet Long u

Listen for the sound of long **u** in **mule**. The letters **u__e** and **ue** usually stand for the long **u** sound.

m**ule**

Directions: Circle the pictures whose names have the long **u** sound.

Search and Color

Directions: Each word in the box has the sound of long **u**. Color the picture that matches each word in the box.

mule	glue	cubes	flute

Name _____

Meet Long o

Listen for the sound of long **o** in **rose**.

Directions: Say the name of each picture. Decide whether the vowel sound you hear is long **o** or short **o**. Fill in the circle beside long **o** or short **o**.

r**o**s**e**

○ Long o   ○ Short o

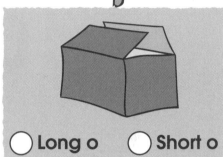

○ Long o   ○ Short o

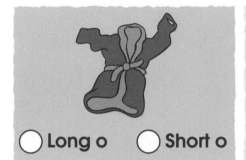

○ Long o   ○ Short o

○ Long o   ○ Short o

○ Long o   ○ Short o

○ Long o   ○ Short o

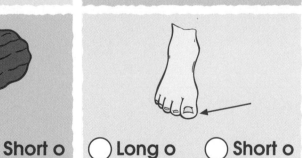

○ Long o   ○ Short o

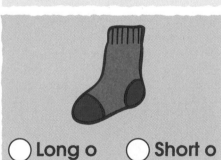

○ Long o   ○ Short o

○ Long o   ○ Short o

○ Long o   ○ Short o

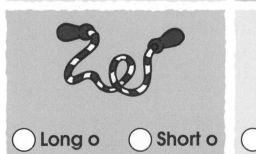

○ Long o   ○ Short o

○ Long o   ○ Short o

Name _____

Meet Long e

Listen for the sound of long **e** in **bee**. The letters **ee** and **ea** usually stand for the long **e** sound.

Directions: Write the name of the picture on the correct line.

b**ee**

seal

ten

beet

jeep

leaf

bed

red

seat

feet

ee	ea	Short Vowel e

Name _____

Long Vowel Puzzles

Directions: Cut out the puzzle pieces. Match each picture with its name.

Name _____

Long Vowel Crossword

Directions: Fill in the puzzle with the correct words.

Across

1.

4.

5.

Down

1.

2.

3.

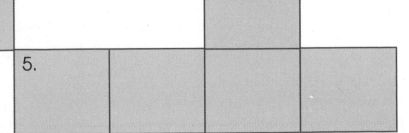

Long Vowels

Vowels are the letters **a**, **e**, **i**, **o**, and **u**. Long vowel sounds say their own names. Long **a** is the sound you hear in **hay**. Long **e** is the sound you hear in **me**. Long **i** is the sound you hear in **pie**. Long **o** is the sound you hear in **no**. Long **u** is the sound you hear in **cute**.

Directions: Say the long vowel sound at the beginning of each row. Say the name of each picture. Color the pictures in each row that have the same long vowel sound as that letter.

ā

ē

ī

ō

ū

Name _____

Long Vowel Sounds

Directions: Write **a**, **e**, **i**, **o**, or **u** in each blank to finish the word. Draw a line from the word to the picture.

c _ _ _ ke

r _ _ _ se

k _ _ te

f _ _ t

m _ _ le

Name _____

Super Silent e

When you add an **e** to the end of some words, the vowel changes from a short vowel sound to a long vowel sound. The **e** is silent.

Example: rip + **e** = ripe.

Directions: Say the word under the first picture in each pair. Then, add an **e** to the word under the next picture. Say the new word.

can

_____

tub

_____

man

_____

kit

_____

pin

_____

cap

_____

Name _____

The Super Silent e

cap + e = cape

Adding **e** to the end of the **short vowel** word **cap** changes it to the **long vowel** word **cape**.

Directions: Cut out the tub. Cut on the dotted lines to make slits. Slip the water through the slits in the tub. Next, cut out the tube. Glue the tube in the tub, but don't glue the cap down. When the cap is on the tube, read the short vowel word. Then, fold the cap back to show the **e**. Read the long vowel word.

Example:

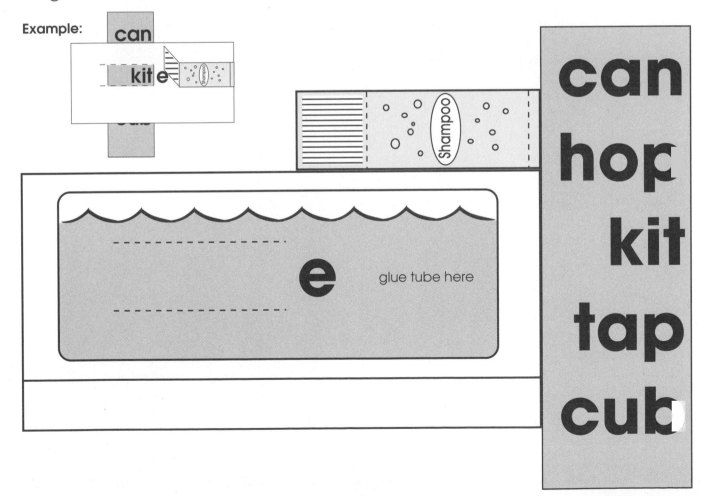

can
kit e
hop
kit
tap
cub

e   glue tube here

Shampoo

Words With Silent e

When a silent **e** appears at the end of a word, you can't hear it, but it makes the other vowel have a **long** sound. For example, **tub** has a **short** vowel sound, and **tube** has a **long** vowel sound.

Directions: Look at the pictures below. Decide if the word has a short or long vowel sound. Circle the correct word. Watch for the silent **e!**

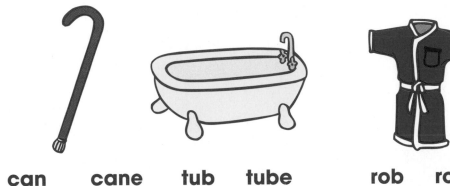

can   cane   tub   tube   rob   robe   rat   rate

pin   pine   cap   cape   not   note   pan   pane

slid   slide   dim   dime   tap   tape   cub   cube

Name _____

Final y as a Vowel

Our puppy stays dry in the yard.

You know that **y** is a consonant. When **y** is at the beginning of a word, it makes the sound at the beginning of **yard**.

Y can also be a vowel.

Sometimes **y** can have the long **e** sound you hear at the end of **puppy**. **Y** has this sound when it is at the end of a word with more than one syllable or part.

Sometimes **y** can have the long **i** sound you hear at the end of **dry**. **Y** has this sound when it is at the end of a one-syllable word.

Directions: Say each picture name. Circle the word that names the picture. If **y** makes the long **e** sound, color the picture brown. If **y** makes the long **i** sound, color the picture orange.

bail
bay
baby

crazy
cry
crate

bunt
bunny
buy

fry
frosty
frog

pay
pry
pony

fly
feed
fussy

Final y as a Vowel

Y at the end of a word is a vowel. When **y** is at the end of a one-syllable word, it has the sound of a long **i** (as in **my**). When **y** is at the end of a word with more than one syllable, it has the sound of a long **e** (as in **baby**).

Directions: Look at the words in the box. If the word has the sound of a long **i**, write it under the word **my**. If the word has the sound of a long **e**, write it under the word **baby**. Write the word from the box that answers each riddle.

happy	penny	try	sleepy	dry
bunny	why	sky	party	fly

my   **baby**

_____   _____

_____   _____

_____   _____

_____   _____

1. It takes five of these to make a nickel.   _____

2. This is what you call a baby rabbit.   _____

3. It is often blue and you can see it if you look up.   _____

4. You might have one of these on your birthday.   _____

5. It is the opposite of wet.   _____

6. You might use this word to ask a question.   _____

7. This is what birds and airplanes can do.   _____

The Sounds of y

A **y** at the end of a word can have the long **i** sound or the long **e** sound. Listen for the long **i** sound in **fly**. Listen for the long **e** sound in **pony**.

fl**y**

pon**y**

Directions: Say the name of each picture. Listen for the sound of **y** at the end of the word. Circle either long **i** or long **e**.

sky

Long i   **Long e**

baby

Long i   **Long e**

bunny

Long i   **Long e**

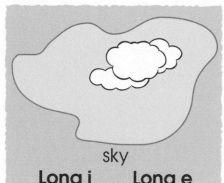

cry

Long i   **Long e**

penny

Long i   **Long e**

muddy

Long i   **Long e**

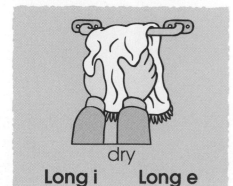

dry

Long i   **Long e**

20

twenty

Long i   **Long e**

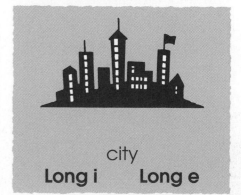

city

Long i   **Long e**

Name _____

Which Sound of y?

Directions: Say the name of each picture. If the final **y** stands for the long **e** sound, color the picture green. If the **y** stands for the long **i** sound, color the picture yellow.

pony

fly

fifty

candy

dry

penny

cherry

sky

bunny

Name _____

Finish-the-Word Puzzles

Directions: Write a vowel in the middle of each puzzle that will make a word across and down.

	w	
p		t
	b	

	m	
d		g
	p	

	f	
m		p
	n	

	w	
p		g
	n	

	h	
b		x
	t	

	b	
s		n
	s	

Name _____

Letter Lift

Directions: Cut out the letters below. Glue each letter on the correct balloon.

w s m a q h d o r j x p y
f g t i l b e n v u c k z

Short and Long Vowel Sounds

Directions: Cut out the pictures below. If the vowel has a **long** sound, glue it on the **long** vowel side. If the vowel has a **short** sound, glue it on the **short** vowel side.

Short | Long

cut ✂ -

| hat | boat | bike | cube | bed |
| pig | beads | cake | pots | truck |

Name _____

Review

Directions: Color all of the vowels black to discover something hidden in the puzzle.

```
j  e  j  g  w  d  q  n  j  c  g  c  u  b
k  g  u  m  b  j  h  c  h  w  l  o  d  s
r  c  z  i  l  p  q  s  b  k  i  n  z  f
g  k  w  x  e  d  a  e  f  e  l  x  q  k
v  r  f  j  p  i  o  u  a  g  n  f  s  b
d  n  v  m  a  e  e  i  u  u  h  b  s  f
u  a  e  i  e  u  a  i  u  e  a  e  i  u
l  z  k  i  u  u  a  a  e  e  i  m  w  z
q  h  r  a  e  u  e  i  a  e  e  c  c  b
i  u  u  e  o  a  o  u  o  i  i  o  o  u
t  x  b  h  a  i  e  o  u  a  d  v  r  l
c  h  f  s  j  e  i  e  i  f  f  k  j  v
n  m  d  t  e  g  a  o  t  i  j  m  x  h
t  p  g  i  c  v  h  n  g  d  o  p  r  l
l  h  o  k  q  f  r  p  s  j  t  u  g  v
```

What was hidden?

_____

Name _____

Review

Directions: Circle the word if it has a long vowel sound.

Remember: A long vowel says its name.

feet

snake

cup

hose

tie

hat

dog

rake

bug

bone

bib

net

Name _____

Review

Directions: Write a vowel on each line to complete each word.

a   e   i   o   u

 c__t

 b__k__

 sm__k__

tr____

 c__b

p__n

 m__m

b__b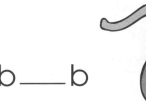

 d__d

d__ck

Name _____

Short and Long Vowels

Directions: Say the name of each picture. Write the vowel on each line that completes the word. Color the short vowel pictures. Circle the long vowel pictures.

a e i o u

 j _____ g

 t _____ pe

 l _____ af

 p _____ n

 l _____ ck

 c _____ t

 c _____ be

 b _____ ll

 k _____ te

 r _____ pe

Name _____

Consonant Blends With r

Sometimes two consonants at the beginning of a word blend together. Listen for the **dr** blend in **dragon**. **Gr**, **fr**, **cr**, **tr**, **br**, and **pr** are also **r** blends.

dragon

Directions: Draw a line from each consonant blend to the picture whose name begins with the same sound.

dr

br

cr

tr

pr

gr

fr

Name _____

Fill the Tray

Directions: Read the menu. Circle the words that have **r** blends. On the tray, draw pictures of the foods whose names you circled.

bread	pretzel	meat
butter	milk	grapes
salad	french fries	ice cream

Name _____

Consonant Blends With l

Listen for the **cl** blend in **clown**. **Gl, pl, fl,** and **bl** are also **l** blends.

clown

Directions: Look at the **l** blend at the beginning of each row. Color the picture whose name begins with that sound.

bl

cl

fl

gl

pl

Name _____

Tic-Tac-Toe With l Blends

Directions: Color the pictures whose names begin with **l** blends. Draw a line through three colored pictures in a row to score a Tic-Tac-Toe.

96

Name _____

Consonant Blends With s

Listen for the **sk** blend in **skunk**. **Sm**, **st**, **sp**, **sw**, **sc**, **squ**, **sl**, and **sn** are also **s** blends.

skunk

Directions: Say the name of each picture. Circle the **s** blend you hear at the beginning of the name.

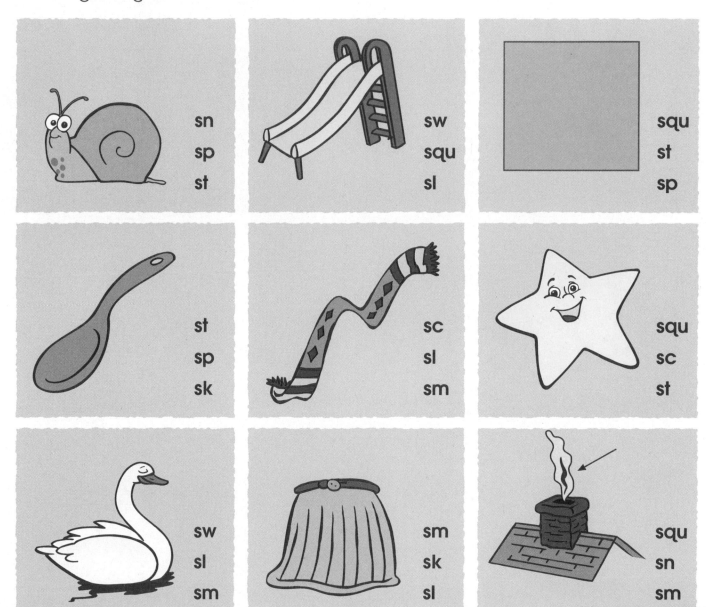

sn
sp
st

sw
squ
sl

squ
st
sp

st
sp
sk

sc
sl
sm

squ
sc
st

sw
sl
sm

sm
sk
sl

squ
sn
sm

Name _____

Match Pictures and Blends

Directions: Draw a line from each **s** blend to the picture whose name begins with that sound.

squ

sp

sw

sl

sk

sn

st

sm

98

Name _____

Blends at the Ends

Some consonant blends come at the ends of words.
Listen for the **nd** blend at the end of the word **round**.
Mp, **ng**, **nt**, **sk**, **nk**, and **st** can also be ending blends.

rou**nd**

Directions: Say the name of each picture. Circle the blend you hear at
the end of the name.

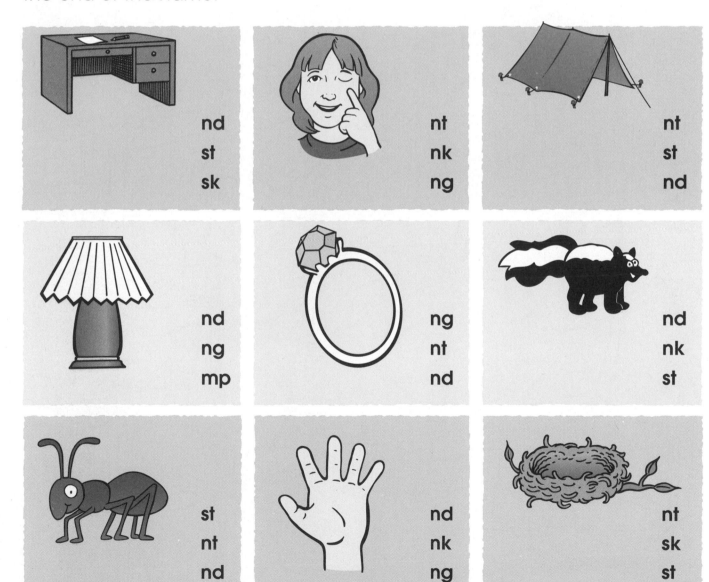

nd
st
sk

nt
nk
ng

nt
st
nd

nd
ng
mp

ng
nt
nd

nd
nk
st

st
nt
nd

nd
nk
ng

nt
sk
st

Name _____

Follow the Final Blends

Directions: Find the notes with pictures whose names end with consonant blends. Color them yellow. Draw a line through the yellow notes from the band to the tent.

Consonant Blends

Name _____

Ending Consonant Blends

Directions: Write **lt** or **ft** to complete the words.

_____

- - - - - - - - - - - - - - -

be _____

_____

- - - - - - - - - - - - - - -

ra _____

_____

- - - - - - - - - - - - - - -

sa _____

_____

- - - - - - - - - - - - - - -

qui _____

_____

- - - - - - - - - - - - - - -

le _____

Name _____

Ending Consonant Blends

Directions: Draw a line from the picture to the blend that ends the word.

lf

lk

sk

st

Name _____

Ending Consonant Blends

Directions: Every jukebox has a word ending and a list of letters. Add each of the letters to the word ending to make rhyming words.

_____ and

b _____
h _____
l _____
s _____

_____ ent

b _____
d _____
t _____
w _____

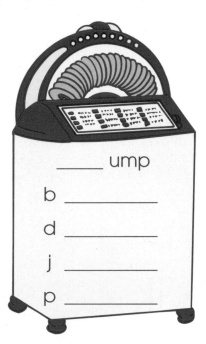

_____ ump

b _____
d _____
j _____
p _____

_____ ink

p _____
s _____
l _____
th _____

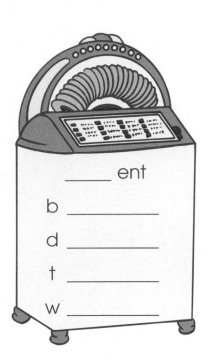

_____ ing

r _____
s _____
st _____
k _____

_____ ank

b _____
r _____
s _____
t _____

Name _____

Ending Consonant Blends

Directions: Say the blend for each word as you search for it. Circle the letters that make each word.

```
b  e  l  t  l  e  m  m  i  l  k  r  p
b  r  l  z  m  a  a  i  u  v  r  i  n
r  r  d  u  m  p  s  h  n  x  i  t  a
i  b  p  i  n  g  k  p  i  b  n  g  w
n  m  k  i  q  i  w  e  n  t  g  d  s
g  t  h  i  n  k  n  c  e  s  i  r  h
e  e  i  k  i  f  h  r  c  d  x  e  e
t  c  s  j  b  c  l  a  s  p  n  m  l
e  r  i  e  l  o  m  n  i  y  e  p  f
n  b  n  b  a  n  d  k  g  o  s  f  k
t  a  g  l  n  a  l  a  n  d  t  e  d
x  d  c  o  k  u  z  j  e  l  u  m  p
r  a  f  t  b  r  h  s  h  r  i  n  k
```

Words to find:

belt	raft	milk	shelf
mask	clasp	nest	band
think	went	lump	crank
ring	blank	shrink	land
bring	tent	dump	sing

Review

Directions: Complete each sentence with a word from the word box.

| sting | shelf | drank | plant | stamp |

1. Tom _____ his milk.

2. A bee can _____ you.

3. I put a _____ on my letter.

4. The _____ is green.

5. The book is on the _____ .

Missing Blends

Directions: Fill in the circle beside the missing blend in each word.

__ain	__an	te__
◯ sk	◯ sl	◯ sk
◯ tr	◯ sm	◯ nt
◯ pr	◯ sw	◯ ng

__ate	__ate	__ide
◯ sk	◯ pl	◯ sk
◯ sm	◯ pr	◯ cl
◯ cr	◯ sp	◯ sl

__ail	__ess	de__
◯ ng	◯ pr	◯ st
◯ sn	◯ dr	◯ nd
◯ st	◯ nd	◯ sk

Name _____

More Missing Blends

Directions: Fill in the circle beside the missing blend in each word.

ri__	__y	__apes
○ nt	○ sl	○ gr
○ st	○ fl	○ cl
○ ng	○ pl	○ sk

__obe	ha__	__og
○ sl	○ nd	○ gr
○ gl	○ ng	○ tr
○ gr	○ sk	○ fr

__y	__ider	la__
○ sk	○ pr	○ st
○ sm	○ sl	○ mp
○ nt	○ sp	○ ng

Name _____

Picture Clues

Directions: Read the sentence. Circle the word that makes sense. Use the picture clues to help you. Then, write the word.

I ride on a _____.
bike   hike

I ride on a _____.
train   tree

I ride in a _____.
car   can

I ride on a _____.
bus   bug

I ride in a _____.
jar   jet

I ride in a _____.
took   truck

Name _____

Picture Clues

Directions: Cut out the pictures below. Glue them next to the sentences that tell about them.

The sun is yellow.

It is raining.

The boy can grin.

The bed is broken.

My pen and paper are here.

Cut

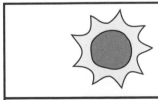 

Picture Clues

Directions: Read the sentence. Circle the word that makes sense. Use the picture clues to help you. Then, write the word.

_____

I see the _____.
bird   book

I see the _____.
fish   fork

I see the _____.
dogs   dig

I see the _____.
cats   coat

I see the _____.
snake   snow

I see the _____.
rat   rake

Name _____

Fun With Directions

Directions: Follow the number code to color the balloons.
Color the clown, too.

1 — blue	2 — orange	3 — yellow	4 — green	5 — purple
6 — brown	7 — red	8 — black	9 — blue	10 — pink

Name _____

Draw With Directions

Directions: Follow the directions to complete the picture.

1. Draw a smiling yellow face on the sun.

2. Color the fish blue. Draw 2 more blue fish in the water.

3. Draw a brown bird under the cloud. Draw blue raindrops under the cloud.

4. Color the boat purple. Color one sail orange. Color the other sail green.

5. Color the starfish yellow. Draw 2 more yellow starfish.

Name _____

Follow the Course

Directions: Tear out page 115. Place a penny in the top left corner. Then, follow the directions below to win the trophy. Check off the directions as you follow them.

1.
- [ ] Go right 7 spaces.
- [ ] Go down 5 spaces.
- [ ] Go left 6 spaces.
- [ ] Go down 4 spaces.
- [ ] Leap through the hoop.

2.
- [ ] Go right 3 spaces.
- [ ] Go up 5 spaces.
- [ ] Go left 4 spaces.
- [ ] Go up 1 space.
- [ ] Do a handstand on your skateboard.

3.
- [ ] Go right 2 spaces.
- [ ] Go up 2 spaces.
- [ ] Go right 3 spaces.
- [ ] Go down 3 spaces.
- [ ] Glide down the ramp.

4.
- [ ] Go right 1 space.
- [ ] Go down 3 spaces.
- [ ] Go left 3 spaces.
- [ ] Go down 2 spaces.
- [ ] Turn the corner.

5.
- [ ] Go right 4 spaces.
- [ ] Go up 8 spaces.
- [ ] Go left 4 spaces.
- [ ] Go down 1 space.
- [ ] Duck! Here's a tunnel.

6.
- [ ] Go left 2 spaces.
- [ ] Go down 6 spaces.
- [ ] Go left 1 space.
- [ ] Go up 2 spaces.
- [ ] You made it! Collect your trophy.

Skateboard Course

Name _____

Directions for Decorating

Directions: Follow the directions to decorate the bedroom.

Draw a red  between the two  .

Draw a 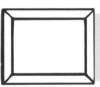 under the window. Color it green.

Draw three big on the wall. Color them orange.

Draw a picture of something you would like to have in your bedroom.

Name _____

Following Directions

Read the sentences. Then, follow the directions.

Directions: Bob is making a snowman. He needs your help. Draw a black hat on the snowman. Draw red buttons. Now, draw a green scarf. Draw a happy face on the snowman.

Name _____

Following Directions

Follow the directions to make a paper sack puppet.

Directions: Find a small sack that fits your hand. Cut out teeth from colored paper. Glue them on the sack. Cut out ears. Glue them on the sack. Cut out eyes, a nose, and a tongue. Glue them all on.

Number the pictures **1**, **2**, **3**, and **4** to show the correct order.

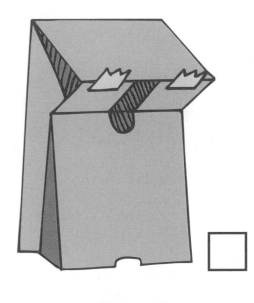

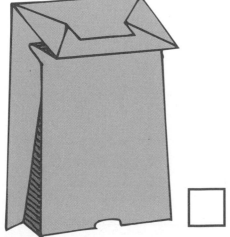

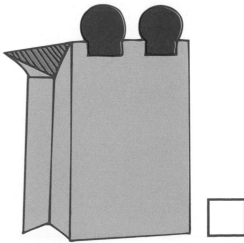

Name _____

Color Code Classifying

Directions: Underline **name words** in **blue**.
Underline **number words** in **red**.
Underline **animal words** in **yellow**.
Underline **color words** in **green**.

pig	Kim	dog	blue
red	green	ten	five
Jack	two	cow	Lee

Directions: Write each word on the correct line.

Name Words

_____   _____   _____

– –

_____   _____   _____

Number Words

_____   _____   _____

– –

_____   _____   _____

Animal Words

_____   _____   _____

– –

_____   _____   _____

Color Words

_____   _____   _____

– –

_____   _____   _____

Name _____

Menu Mix-Up

Directions: Circle **names of drinks** in **red**.
Circle **names of vegetables** in **green**.
Circle **names of desserts** in **pink**.

water

corn
_____
peas

pie

cookie

carrot
_____
cake

juice

milk

Directions: Write each food word on the correct line.

Drinks	Vegetables	Desserts

Name _____

Word Sort

Directions: Circle words that name **colors** in **red**.
Circle words that name **shapes** in **yellow**.
Circle words that name **numbers** in **green**.

five   blue

ten

square   circle

nine

purple

triangle

brown

Directions: Write each word on the correct line.

Colors	Shapes	Numbers

122

Name _____

Sort It Out

Directions: Color the pictures. Cut out and glue each picture in the correct room.

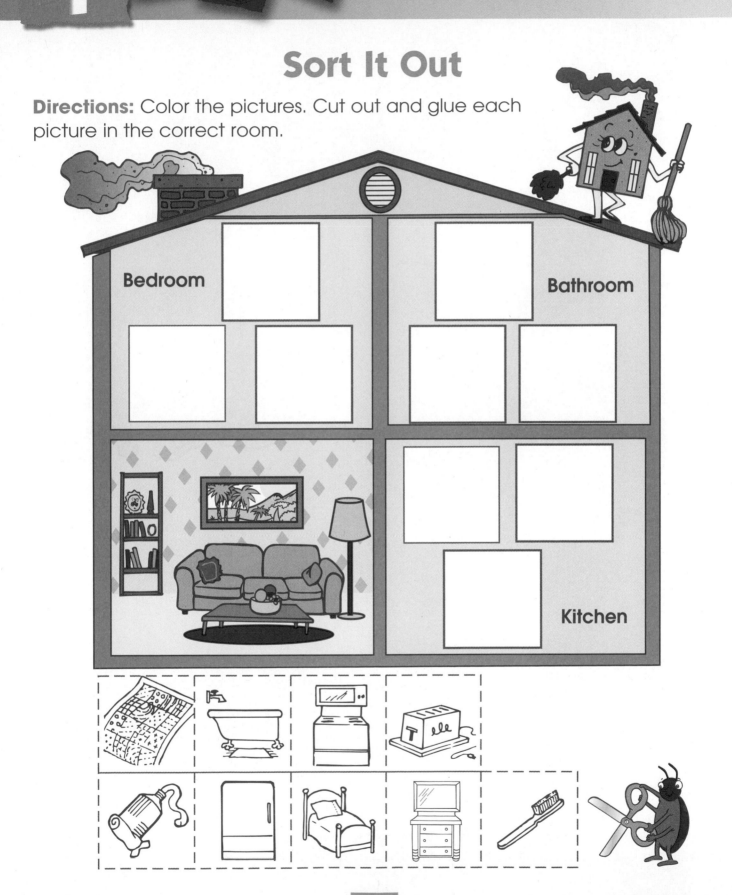

Name _____

Where Does It Belong?

Directions: Read the words.
Draw a **circle** around the **sky words**.
Draw a **line** under the **land words**.
Draw a **box** around the **sea words**.

city	rabbit	planet
cloud	forest	whale
shark	moon	shell

Directions: Write each word on the correct line.

Sky Words

_____ _____ _____

_ _ _ _ _ _ _ _   _ _ _ _ _ _ _ _   _ _ _ _ _ _ _ _

_____ _____ _____

Land Words

_____ _____ _____

_ _ _ _ _ _ _ _   _ _ _ _ _ _ _ _   _ _ _ _ _ _ _ _

_____ _____ _____

Sea Words

_____ _____ _____

_ _ _ _ _ _ _ _   _ _ _ _ _ _ _ _   _ _ _ _ _ _ _ _

Name _____

Classification

Directions: Draw an **X** on the picture that does **not** belong in each group.

Fruit

apple

peach

corn

watermelon

Wild Animals

bear

kitten

gorilla

lion

Pets

cat

goldfish

elephant

dog

Flowers

grass

rose

daisy

tulip

Name _____

Classification

Directions: Dapper Dog is going on a camping trip. Draw an **X** on the word in each row that does **not** belong.

I.	flashlight	candle	radio	fire
2.	shirt	pants	coat	bat
3.	cow	car	bus	train
4.	beans	hot dog	ball	bread
5.	gloves	hat	book	boots
6.	fork	butter	cup	plate
7.	book	ball	bat	milk
8.	dogs	bees	flies	ants

Name _____

Classification

Directions: The words in each box form a group. Choose the word from the box that describes each group and write it on the line.

clothes	family	colors	flowers
fruits	animals	coins	toys	noises

rose
buttercup
tulip
daisy

_____

crash
bang
ring
pop

_____

mother
father
sister
brother

_____

puzzle
wagon
blocks
doll

_____

green
purple
blue
red

_____

grapes
orange
apple
plum

_____

shirt
socks
dress
coat

_____

dime
penny
nickel
quarter

_____

dog
horse
elephant
moose

_____

Things That Go Together

Directions: Draw a line to connect the things that go together.

toothpaste

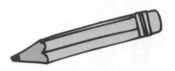

pencil

salt

shoe

soap

pillow

washcloth

sock

toothbrush

pepper

paper

bed

Name _____

More Things That Go Together

Directions: Draw a line to connect the things that go together.

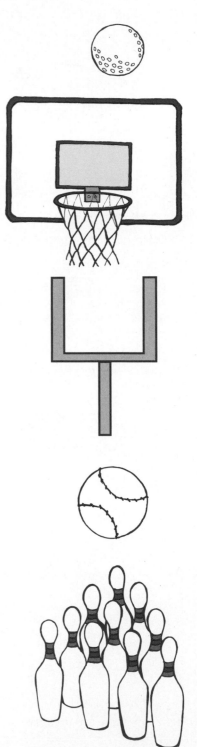

130

Classifying

Name _____

Same and Different

Reading to find out how things are alike or different can help you picture and remember what you read. Things that are alike are called **similarities**. Things that are not alike are called **differences**.

Similarity: Beth and Michelle are both girls.
Difference: Beth has short hair, but Michelle has long hair.

Directions: Read the story.

Michelle and Beth are wearing new dresses. Both dresses are striped and have four shiny buttons. Each dress has a belt and a pocket. Beth's dress is blue and white, while Michelle's is yellow and white. The stripes on Beth's dress go up and down. Stripes on Michelle's dress go from side to side. Beth's pocket is bigger with room for a kitten.

Directions: Add the details. Color the dresses. Show how the dresses are alike and how they are different.

Beth's Dress

Michelle's Dress

Name _____

Comparing Cars

Directions: Read the story.

Sarah built a car for a race. Sarah's car has wheels, a steering wheel, and a place to sit just like the family car. It doesn't have a motor, a key, or a gas pedal. Sarah came in second in last year's race. This year, she hopes to win the race.

Directions: Write **S** beside the things Sarah's car has that are like things the family car has. Write **D** beside the things that are different.

_____		steering wheel
_____		motor
_____		gas pedal
_____		seat
_____		wheels

Name _____

Alike and Different

A Cut-and-Fold Book

Directions: The pages of your Cut-and-Fold Book are on the back of this sheet. First, follow the directions below to make the book. Then, read your book to a family member or friend. Think of other things that are alike and different.

1. Tear the page out of the book.

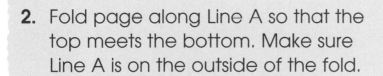

2. Fold page along Line A so that the top meets the bottom. Make sure Line A is on the outside of the fold.

3. Fold along Line B to make the book.

3

He is sad.

He is happy.

Line B

Line A

2

She is short.

She is tall.

4

The elephant is big.

The mouse is little.

ALIKE AND DIFFERENT
A CUT-AND-FOLD BOOK

1

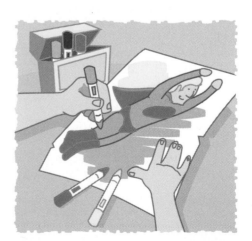

Sequencing Pictures

Directions: Put the pictures in each column in order. Write **1**, **2**, or **3** next to each picture.

Name _____

Sequencing Patterns

Directions: Look for a pattern of shapes inside each pencil. Choose a shape from the picture bank and draw what comes next on each pencil. Then, write the name of the shape on the line.

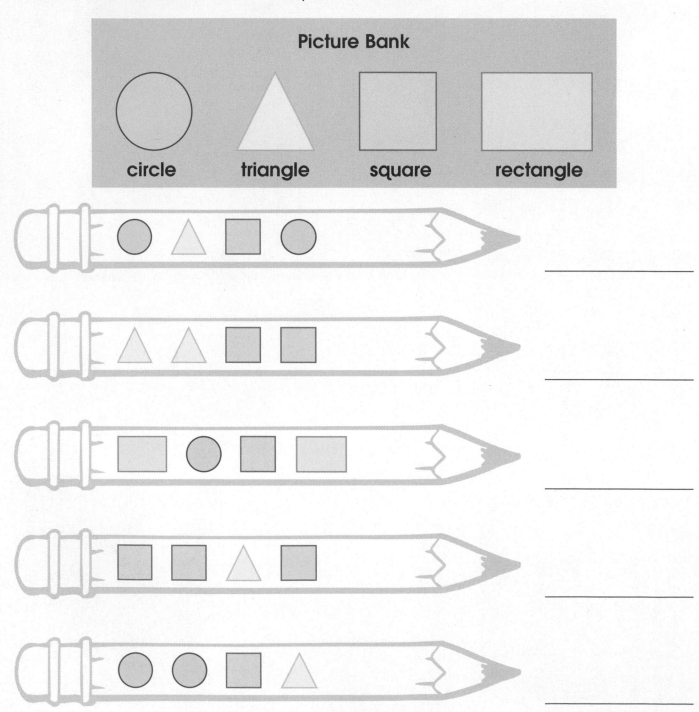

Picture Bank

circle   triangle   square   rectangle

Name _____

Sequencing Riddles

Directions: To solve the riddles below, look at the letter underneath each line. Next, write the letter that comes **before** each letter.

How do you catch a squirrel?

___ ___ ___ ___ ___   ___ ___   ___   ___ ___ ___ ___
D   M   J   N   C   V   Q   B   U   S   F   F

___ ___ ___   ___ ___ ___   ___ ___ ___ ___   ___   ___ ___ ___.
B   O   E   B   D   U   M   J   L   F   B   O   V   U

What has four wheels and flies?

___   ___ ___ ___ ___ ___ ___ ___
B   H   B   S   C   B   H   F

___ ___ ___ ___ ___
U   S   V   D   L

Why did the boy run around his bed?

___ ___   ___ ___ ___ ___ ___   ___ ___   ___ ___
U   P   D   B   U   D   I   V   Q   P   O

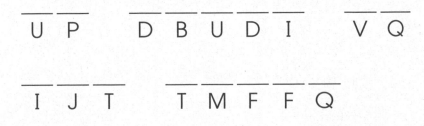

___ ___ ___   ___ ___ ___ ___ ___
I   J   T   T   M   F   F   Q

Name _____

Story Time

Directions: Write each group of sentences in the correct order.

My cat was full and went to sleep.   My cat was hungry.
I filled a bowl with cat food.

1. _____

2. _____

3. _____

I got a gold star.   I studied for my spelling test.
My teacher gave us a list of spelling words.

1. _____

2. _____

3. _____

Name _____

Sequencing

Directions: Look at the picture story. Read the sentences. Then, write **1**, **2**, **3**, or **4** by each sentence to show the order of the story.

Ben rides the bus._____   Ben leaves his house._____

Ben is at the bus stop._____   Ben gets on the bus._____

Name _____

Comprehension: Sequencing

Directions: Kate is sick. What do you think happened? Put numbers beside each sentence to tell the story.

_____ She went to the doctor's office.

_____ Kate felt much better.

_____ Kate felt very hot and tired.

_____ Kate's mother went to the drug store.

_____ The doctor looked in Kate's ears.

_____ Kate took a pill.

_____ The doctor gave Kate's mother a piece of paper.

Name _____

Sequencing

Tom and Tess are making a snack. They are fixing nacho chips and cheese.

Directions: Look at the picture. Then, look at the steps that Tom and Tess use. Put numbers beside each sentence to tell the correct order.

_____ Tom and Tess cook the chips in the microwave oven for 2 minutes.

_____ They get out a plate to cook on.

_____ Tom and Tess get out the nacho chips and cheese.

_____ Tom and Tess eat the food.

_____ They put the chips on a plate.

_____ They put cheese on the chips.

Name _____

Boats

Directions: Read about boats. Then, answer the questions.

See the boats! They float on water. Some boats have sails. The wind moves the sails. It makes the boats go. Many people name their sailboats. They paint the name on the side of the boat.

_____

- -

1. What makes sailboats move? _____

_____

- -

2. Where do sailboats float? _____

_____

- -

3. What would you name a sailboat? _____

Name _____

Tigers

Directions: Read about tigers. Then, answer the questions.

Tigers sleep during the day. They hunt at night. Tigers eat meat. They hunt deer. They like to eat wild pigs. If they cannot find meat on land, tigers will eat fish.

1. When do tigers sleep?   night   day

2. Name two things tigers eat.

_____   _____

- - - - - - - - - - -   - - - - - - - - - - -

_____   _____

3. When do tigers hunt?   day   night

Name _____

Where Flowers Grow

Directions: Read about flowers. Then, answer the questions.

Some flowers grow in pots. Many flowers grow in flower beds. Others grow beside the road. Some flowers begin from seeds. They grow into small buds. Then, they open wide and bloom. Flowers are pretty!

1. Name two places flowers grow.

_____ _____

_____ _____

_____

_____

2. Some flowers begin from _____.

_____

_____

3. Then, flowers grow into small _____.

_____

_____

4. Flowers then open wide and _____.

Name _____

Fish Come in Many Colors

Directions: Read about the color of fish. Then, tell the colors and color the fish.

All fish live in water. Fish that live at the top are blue, green, or black. Fish that live down deep are silver or red. The colors make it hard to see the fish.

1. Name three colors of fish that live at the top.

_____   _____   _____

- -

_____   _____   _____

2. Name two colors of fish that live down deep.

_____   _____

- -

_____   _____

3. Color the top fish and the bottom fish the correct colors.

Name _____

Zoo Animal Riddles

Directions: Write the name of the animal that answers each riddle.

bear

camel

zebra

lion

elephant

1. I am big and brown. I sleep all winter. What am I?

   _____

2. I look like a horse with black and white stripes. What am I?

   _____

3. I have one or two humps on my back. Sometimes people ride on me. What am I?

   _____

4. I am a very big animal. I have a long nose called a trunk. What am I?

   _____

5. I have sharp claws and teeth. I am a great big cat. What am I?

   _____

Name _____

Important Signs to Know

Directions: Draw a line from the sign to the sentence that tells about it.

1. If you see this sign, watch out for trains.

2. When cars or bikes come to this sign,
   they must stop.

3. When this sign is on, do not cross the street.

4. This sign tells you to stay out of the yard.

5. If you see this sign, do not eat or drink
   what is inside!

6. This sign warns you that it is not safe.
   Stay away!

7. This sign says you are not allowed to
   come in.

Name _____

Comprehension

Directions: Read the story. Write the words from the story that complete each sentence.

Jane and Bill like to play in the rain. They take off their shoes and socks. They splash in the puddles. It feels cold! It is fun to splash!

_____

Jane and Bill like to _____.

_____

They take off their _____.

_____

They splash in _____.

Do you like to splash in puddles?   Yes   No

Name _____

Comprehension

Directions: Read the story. Write the words from the story that complete each sentence.

Ben and Sue have a bug. It is red with black spots. They call it Spot. Spot likes to eat green leaves and grass. The children keep Spot in a box.

_____

Ben and Sue have a _____.

_____

It is _____ with black spots.

_____

The bug's name is _____.

_____

The bug eats _____.

Name _____

What Will Happen Next?

Directions: Look at the pictures.

Directions: Write what you think will happen next.

_____

_____

Name _____

What's Next?

Directions: Draw a picture of what you think will happen next in the boxes below.

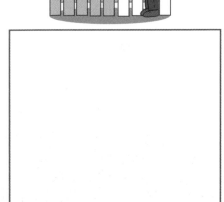

Name _____

What Happens Next?

Directions: Read the story. Predict what will happen and circle your answer choice.

David and Fran go the park. The friendly ice-cream man is there selling ice-cream cones. "Hi kids, would you two like an ice-cream cone?" he asks.

Fran and David reach into their pockets, which are empty. "We don't have any money," says Fran. The ice-cream man smiles at them and reaches into his freezer. Then, he says…

1. Ice cream is bad for children.

2. Today it is my treat. Free ice cream for both of you!

3. I am sorry, maybe next time.

Directions: Draw a picture of what you think will happen.

What Comes Next?

It's fun to try to guess what will happen next as you read. Guessing what will happen is called **predicting outcomes**.

What you read: Liz drops the glass vase.

What you can predict: The glass vase will break.

Directions: Read the story. Then, follow the directions below.

Every Saturday, Grace cleans her room. One Saturday, Grace forgot to clean it because she was busy playing with her cat, Tiger. Mom looked in and saw that Grace's room was still messy.

1. Complete the sentence to make a prediction.

   _____

   _ _ _ _ _ _ _ _ _ _ _ _ _ _

   Now, Grace will probably _____

   _____

   _ _ _ _ _ _ _ _ _ _ _ _ _ _

   _____

2. Color the things Grace will probably hang in her closet.

Name _____

Inside Out!

Directions: Can you match the outsides with the insides? Draw a line from each picture on the left to its inside picture on the right.

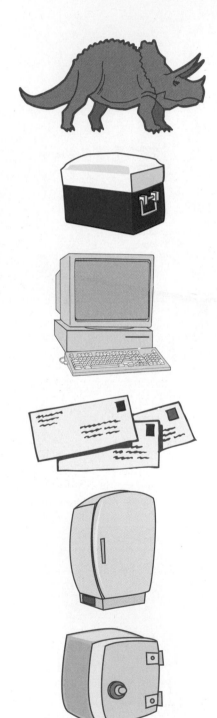

Books for Gabby!

Gabby loves to read books about many different topics. She loves to read about exotic animals. She loves stories about famous people. Gabby is also interested in becoming a doctor or an actress one day.

Directions: Look at the books below. Circle only the books that Gabby would like to read.

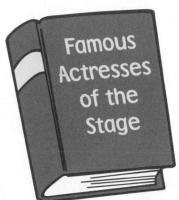

Famous Actresses of the Stage

How to Build a Tree House

Amazing Animals of the Amazon

Baking Muffins With Mom

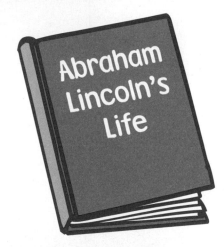

Abraham Lincoln's Life

Spend a Day With a Doctor!

CARTOON CRAZY

Dogs, Cats, and Other Household Pets

Name _____

Use Your Head!

Directions: Read each sentence below. Then, read each statement that follows it. Using the information in the first sentence, decide which word best completes each statement. Then, write that word on the line.

"Please put on your heavy winter coat before you go sledding," said my mom.

My mom wanted me to keep

_____.   cool   warm

I put on my coat _____

I went sledding.   before   after

"Don't forget to bring your glasses, Tom! It will be hard to see the chalkboard if you don't wear them," reminded his dad.

Tom has _____ eyesight.

good   poor

Tom is _____.

forgetful   aware

Tom is going to _____.

school   basketball   practice

Name _____

Where Do I Go?

Directions: Read the sentences below. Then, select words from the word list to write on the lines.

Word List

hospital   bookstore   bakery   park

My mom loves doughnuts. Dad and I wanted to surprise her with some. We stopped at the

_____.

I love to read books! My mom said she would buy me a book at the

_____.

I hurt my ankle at my basketball game. My coach took me to the

_____.

It was a warm summer day, and my family went to the

_____.

Making Inferences

157

Total Reading Grade 1

Name _____

Help Hattie!

Help Hattie pick out birthday presents!

Directions: Read the sentences about her friends. Then, write words from the word list on the lines. Draw a picture of each present inside the boxes.

Word List

music	airplane	goggles
crayons	journal	

 Nancy loves to color pictures.

_____

 Ray wants to be a pilot.

_____

 Kristin loves to write.

_____

 Jared swims every week.

_____

 Chelsea is a great piano player.

_____

Name _____

Critical Thinking

Directions: Use your reading skills to answer each riddle. Unscramble the word to check your answer. Write the correct word on the line.

I am a ruler, but I have two feet, not one.

_____

‒ ‒ ‒ ‒ ‒ ‒

I am a _____ .

(ngik)

I am very bright, but that doesn't make me smart.

_____

‒ ‒ ‒ ‒ ‒ ‒ ·

I am the _____ .

(uns)

You can turn me around, but I won't get dizzy.

_____

‒ ‒ ‒ ‒ ‒ ‒ ‒

I am a _____ .

(eky)

I can rattle, but I am not a baby's toy.

_____

‒ ‒ ‒ ‒ ‒ ‒

I am a _____ .

(nekas)

I will give you milk, but not in a bottle.

_____

‒ ‒ ‒ ‒ ‒ ‒

I am a _____ .

(ocw)

I smell, but I have no nose.

_____

‒ ‒ ‒ ‒ ‒ ‒ ‒

I am a _____ .

(oerflw)

Name _____

Clues About Cats

Directions: Read the clues carefully. Then, number the cats. When you are sure you are correct, color the cats.

1. A gray cat sits on the gate.

2. A cat with orange-and-black spots sits near the tree.

3. A brown cat sits near the bush.

4. A white cat sits between the orange-and-black spotted cat and the gray cat.

5. A black cat sits next to the brown cat.

6. An orange cat sits between the gray cat and the black cat.

Critical Thinking

GREAT JOB!

COOL!

Fantastic!

WOW!

WAY TO GO!

Hidden Meanings

Directions: Cut out the cards. Use your thinking skills to match the picture words with their meanings.

WALKING

R U R
U N N
G the block
N N
I

T
O
U
C
H

he♥art

broken
heart

TIRE

R   R
O O
A
D D
S   S

walking tall

touchdown

crossroads

flat tire

running
around
the block

Name _____

Hey! What's the Big Idea?

Directions: Circle the words that are shown in the picture above.

bowl	spatula	bed	dog	ink
oven	pan	jar	pot	phone
mixer	napkins	scooter	girl	sneakers
mitt	paper towels	car	socks	cupcake tin
spoon		cat	milk	

Directions: Circle and write the best title for the picture.

Baking With Dad   Chocolate Attack!   Eating Food

_____

Tell why the other two titles are not as good.

_____

_____

Name _____

Picture This!

Directions: Look at the picture. Circle and write the best title on the lines below.

B-r-r-r, It's Cold!   Bears and Birds

Asleep for the Winter   Bears Go Shopping

_____

_____

Fishing   Our New Fish

The Pet Store   Fish and Chips

_____

_____

Spring Cleaning   My New Toy

Saturday Fun   New Shoes

_____

_____

Picture This!

Directions: Write a title beside each picture below. Your title should tell what each picture is about in just a few words.

_____

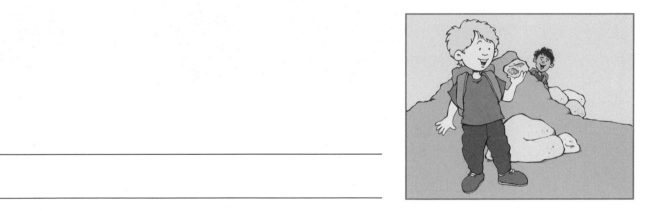

_____

_____

Name _____

What's the Main Idea?

The **main idea** tells about the **whole picture**.

Directions: Does the sentence tell the main idea of the picture? Circle **yes** or **no**. Then, write the sentence that best states the main idea for each picture.

The cat wants to play.   yes   no

The cat takes a nap.   yes   no

_____

_____

The brothers play together.   yes   no

The brothers are smart.   yes   no

_____

_____

The dog is hungry.   yes   no

The dog is playful.   yes   no

_____

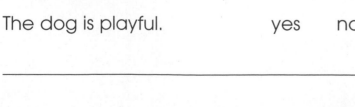

_____

Name _____

Story Time

The **main idea** tells about the **whole story**.

Read the story below.

"Mom, can we build a fort in the dining room?" John asked.

"Sure, honey," said John's mom. Then, John's mom covered the dining room table with a giant sheet. "Do you want to eat lunch in our fort?" asked John's mom.

"Yes!" said John. Then, John's mom brought two peanut butter sandwiches on paper plates and sat under the table, too!

"Mom, making a fort with you is so much fun!" said John, smiling.

Directions: Does the sentence tell the main idea? Write **yes** or **no**.

1. Then, John's mom covered the dining room table with a giant sheet. _____

2. "Do you want to eat lunch in our fort?" asked John's mom.

   _____

3. "Mom, making a fort with you is so much fun!" _____

4. Write a sentence that tells the main idea: _____

_____

Name _____

Caitlin Uses Context Clues

When you read, it is important to know about context clues. **Context clues** can help you figure out the meaning of a word or a missing word just by looking at the **other words** in the sentence.

Directions: Read each sentence below. Circle the context clues, or other words in the sentence that give you hints about the meaning. Choose the answer that fits in each blank. Write it on the line. The first one is done for you.

It was so (hot) outside that I decided I would go to the (beach) and _____**swim**_____.

    play   laugh   shovel   swim

"Swim" is the correct answer because of the context clues "hot" and "beach." Now you try.

I. Last night I went to bed very late and now I feel _____.

    happy   hungry   tired   yawn

2. When I broke my mom's favorite vase she was _____.

    worried   nice   magic   angry

3. The clown looked very _____ wearing a tiny pink tutu!

    silly   smart   orange   light

Name _____

Caitlin Uses More Context Clues

When you read, it is important to know about context clues. **Context clues** can help you figure out the missing word in a sentence, just by looking at the **other words** in the sentence.

Directions: Read each sentence below. Circle the context clues. Choose the answer that fits in each blank. Write it on the line.

1. The cold wind and lack of heat made me wish

   I had an extra _____.

   umbrella   toy   shovel   jacket

2. A whale is a very _____ mammal. Sailors often thought whales were actually small islands!

   small   graceful   large   blue

3. Eating fruit is important for _____
   health. Fruit is full of many important vitamins.

   bad   good   okay   cat

4. The bus was very large and had a lot of seats. It could carry

   _____ people.

   few   hungry   many   tired

Name _____

Carlo's Context Clues

Context clues can help you figure out the meaning of a word just by looking at the **other words** in the sentence.

Directions: Read each sentence below. Circle the context clues. Choose a word from the word list to replace each word in **bold**. Write it on the line.

	Word List	
stop	shined	tease
smart	lively	yummy

1. This prize-winning chocolate cream pie is **delicious**. _____

2. Please do not **taunt** your younger brother. Mean words hurt his feelings. _____

3. The police officer told us to **halt** when we came to the red traffic light. _____

4. The bouncy, happy puppy was very **energetic**. _____

5. The silver bowl really **gleamed** after you polished it. _____

6. The **intelligent** girl always got 100's on her spelling tests. _____

Name _____

Carlo's Context Clues Continued

Context clues can help you figure out the meaning of a word just by looking at the **other words** in the sentence.

Directions: Read each sentence below. Circle the context clues. Choose a word from the word list to replace each word in **bold**. Write it on the line.

Word List

petted	understand	tell
little	yelled	

1. "Don't **reveal** the secret! We want the party to be a surprise!" said Mary. _____

2. I can't **grasp** that hard math problem! It is too difficult. _____

3. The baby bird was so **tiny** that we could hardly see it. _____

4. We **stroked** the soft kitten and heard it purr. _____

5. The crowd **hollered** when the player was called out. _____

Name _____

What Is Cause and Effect?

Cause: An action or act that makes something happen.

Effect: Something that happens because of an action or cause.

Look at the following example of cause and effect.

Kyle has a spelling test and studies hard.

Kyle's hard work helps him do a super job!

Directions: Now, draw a line connecting each cause on the left side of the page to its effect on the right side of the page.

Name _____

More Cause and Effect!

Cause: An action or act that makes something happen.

Effect: Something that happens because of an action or cause.

Look at the following example of cause and effect.

Directions: Now, draw a line connecting each cause on the left side of the page to its effect on the right side of the page.

Name _____

We Go Together!

Directions: Draw a line connecting the pictures that go together. Then, figure out which picture is the cause and which is the effect. Write **C** for **cause** or **E** for **effect** under each picture.

Name _____

Realistic Story or Fantasy?

Many stories are made-up stories. A made-up story about things that could really happen is a **realistic story**. Some made-up stories, such as fairy tales, tell about things that could never really happen. Those stories are **fantasies**.

Realistic story: A girl hits a home run and wins the game for her team.

Fantasy: A girl hits the ball. It sprouts wings and flies away on an adventure.

Directions: Read the book reviews. Fill in the circle to show whether each story is a realistic story or a fantasy.

The Flying Hippo is about a hippo that flies through the sky. He lands at a busy airport and wanders through New York City.

○ Realistic story   ○ Fantasy

A Goose Learns to Fly is about a family who saves an injured baby goose. Later, they teach it to fly on its own.

○ Realistic story   ○ Fantasy

The First Airplane is about the Wright Brothers and the airplane they invented.

○ Realistic story   ○ Fantasy

The Magic Airplane is about a toy airplane that flies to the planet Mars.

○ Realistic story   ○ Fantasy

Name _____

Fantasy Tales

If even one thing in a story could not really happen, the whole story is a fantasy.

Directions: Read the stories. Underline the sentence that makes each story a fantasy.

Michelle got a kitten for her birthday. It was soft and cuddly. It liked to chase fuzzy toys. After playing, it napped in Michelle's lap. One day, the kitten said to Michelle, "Would you like me to tell you a story?"

The team lined up. The kicker kicked the football. Up, up it soared. It went up so high that it went into orbit around the Earth. The game was over. The Aardvarks had won.

"This is a great car," the salesperson said. "It can go very fast. It can cook your breakfast. It always starts, even on the coldest day. You really should buy this car."

Chris studied about healthy food in school. He learned that milk could make him grow. Chris drank a glass of milk just before he went to bed. When he got up in the morning, he was so tall, his head went right through the ceiling.

Name _____

Write About Reality

Directions: Write a journal entry. Write about a special day. You can make up the story, but make sure everything you write is something that could really happen.

_____

- - - - - - - - - - - - - - - -

_____

- - - - - - - - - - - - - - - -

_____

_____

_____

- - - - - - - - - - - - - - - -

_____

_____

- - - - - - - - - - - - - - - -

_____

_____

- - - - - - - - - - - - - - - -

Name _____

Write a Fantasy

Directions: Write a new journal entry. Write about the same special day you wrote about on page 177. This time, add details to make your story a fantasy.

_____

- -

_____

- -

_____

- -

_____

- -

_____

- -

_____

- -

_____

Name _____

Penguins

A penguin is a bird that cannot fly. Its wings look and act like flippers. Penguins are very good swimmers and spend a lot of time in the water. White belly feathers and short black feathers on their backs make it hard to spot them in the water. They waddle when they walk. Most wild penguins live in the southern part of the world.

Female penguins lay one to three eggs. The male carries the eggs on his feet and covers them with rolls of body fat to keep them warm. A baby penguin is called a *chick* when it is hatched. Most penguins can live for almost twenty years.

Directions: After reading about penguins, decide if each statement is a fact or an opinion. Write **F** for fact and **O** for opinion.

_____ 1. A penguin is a beautiful bird.

_____ 2. A penguin is a bird that cannot fly.

_____ 3. Penguins are good swimmers.

_____ 4. Baby penguins are called *chicks*.

_____ 5. Female penguins are good nest builders.

_____ 6. It is fun to watch penguins swimming.

_____ 7. Bird watchers like to watch penguins.

_____ 8. A penguin may live for twenty years.

Starfish

A starfish is not really a fish. It is an animal. It belongs to a group of animals that have skin that is tough and covered with sharp bumps called *spines*.

Starfish live in the ocean.

Most starfish have five "arms" going out from the main body. This makes them look like stars. The mouth of a starfish is on the underside of its body. A starfish can eat in two different ways. It can take food in through its mouth and eat it. It can also eat by pushing its stomach out of its mouth and wrapping it around the food.

If an arm breaks off the starfish, it can grow a new one.

Directions: Read the statements. Decide if each is a fact or an opinion. Write **F** for fact and **O** for opinion.

_____ **1.** It would be fun to feel a starfish.

_____ **2.** A starfish would be a good pet.

_____ **3.** If a starfish "arm" breaks off, it can grow a new one.

_____ **4.** Starfish look pretty.

_____ **5.** Starfish live in the ocean.

_____ **6.** Starfish have tough skin with spines.

Name _____

Figs

Fig is the name of a fruit and of the plant the fruit grows on. The plant can look like a bush or like a tree. Fig plants grow where it is warm all year long.

The fig fruit grows in bunches on the stems of fig plants. Some figs can be picked two times each year.

They can be picked from old branches in June or July. They can be picked from new branches in August or September.

Many people like to eat figs. They can be eaten in fig cookies or in fig bars. They can be canned or eaten fresh. Sometimes figs are dried.

Directions: Color the fig **red** if the sentence is a **fact**. Color the fig **blue** if the sentence is an **opinion**.

 1. A fig is a plant and a fruit.

 2. The fig tree is very pretty.

 3. Fig plants do not grow where it is very cold.

 4. Figs grow in a bunch.

 5. You can pick figs two times each year.

 6. Figs taste very good.

 7. You can eat figs in many ways.

 8. The best way to eat a fig is in a fig cookie.

Name _____

What's My Name?

Different words have different jobs. A **naming word** names a person, place, or thing. Naming words are also called **nouns**.

Example: person — nurse
place — store
thing — drum

Directions: In the word box below, circle only the words that name a person, place, or thing. Then, use the nouns you circled to name each picture.

teacher	up	dog	the	library
runs	is	cowhand	cap	zoo

182

Name _____

Person, Place, or Thing?

Directions: Write each noun in the correct box below.

girl	park	truck	vase
artist	tree	doctor	zoo
school	store	ball	baby

Person

Place

Thing

Finding Nouns

A **noun** names a person, place, or thing.

Directions: Circle two nouns in each sentence below. The first one is done for you.

The (pig) has a curly (tail.)

The hen is sitting on her nest.

A horse is in the barn.

The goat has horns.

The cow has a calf.

The farmer is painting the fence.

Name _____

Nouns at Play

Directions: Complete each sentence with the correct noun from the word box. Write the noun on the line.

ducks	sun	tree
dog	boys	bird

1. A big _____ grows in the park.

2. The _____ is in the sky.

3. A _____ digs a hole.

4. Three _____ swim in the water.

5. A _____ sits on its nest.

6. Two _____ fly a kite.

Name _____

Nouns

Directions: Complete each sentence with a noun.

_____

1. The _____ is fat.

_____

2. My _____ is blue.

_____

3. The _____ has apples.

_____

4. The _____ is hot.

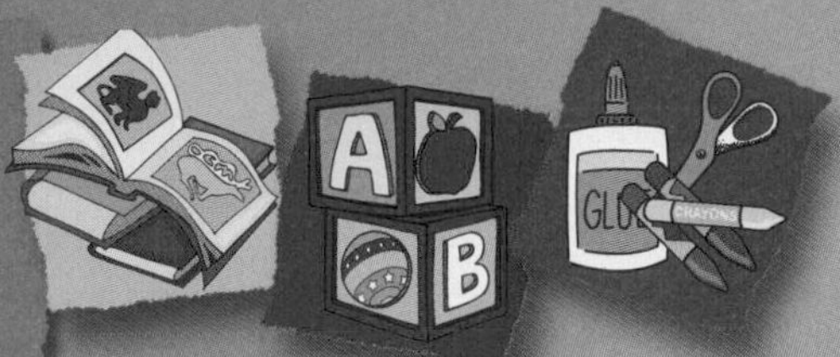

Name ______________________

Nouns

Directions: Write these naming words in the correct box.

store	**zoo**	**child**	**baby**	**teacher**	**table**
cat	**park**	**gym**	**woman**	**sock**	**horse**

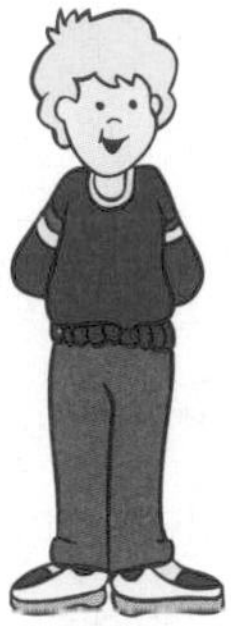

Person

______________________ ______________________

______________________ ______________________

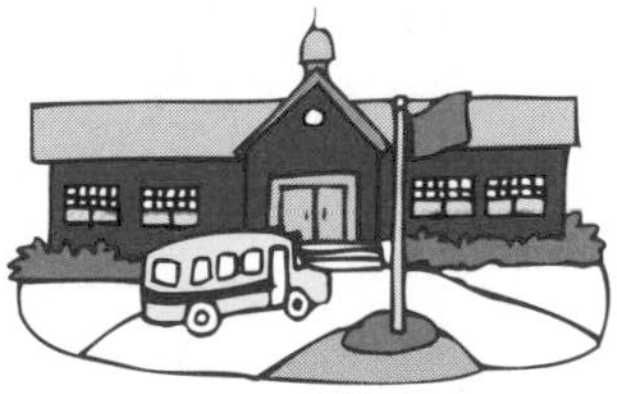

Place

______________________ ______________________

______________________ ______________________

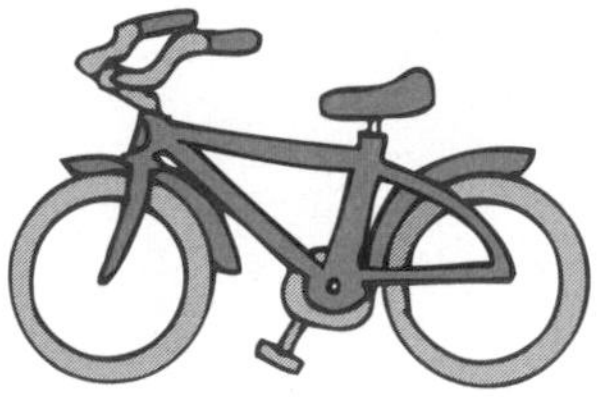

Thing

______________________ ______________________

______________________ ______________________

Name _____

Verbs

Directions: Look at the picture and read the words. Write an action word in each sentence below.

swing

rings

kick

run

talk

1. The two boys like to _____ together.

2. The children _____ the soccer ball.

3. Some children like to _____ on the swing.

4. The girl can _____ very fast.

5. The teacher _____ the bell.

Name _____

Ready, Set, Go!

An **action word** tells what a person or thing can do.

Example: Fred **kicks** the ball.

Directions: Read the words below. Circle words that tell what the children are doing.

jump

boy

sleep

bed

hello

talk

skate

mittens

hop

sidewalk

sing

song

swim

deep

story

read

Name _____

Action Words

Directions: Underline the action word in each sentence. Then, draw a line to match each sentence with the correct picture. The first one is done for you.

The dog <u>barks</u>.

The birds fly.

A fish swims.

A monkey swings.

A turtle crawls.

A boy talks.

What Is a Verb?

A **verb** is an action word. A verb tells what a person or thing does.

Example: Jane **reads** a book.

Directions: Circle the verb in each sentence below.

Two tiny dogs dance.

The bear climbs a ladder.

The clown falls down.

A tiger jumps through a ring.

A boy eats popcorn.

A woman swings on a trapeze.

Name _____

Review

Directions: Read the sentences below. Draw a **red** circle around the **nouns**. Draw a **blue** line under the verbs.

1. The boy runs fast.

2. The turtle eats leaves.

3. The fish swim in the tank.

4. The girl hits the ball.

Name _____

Review

Directions: Cut out the words below. Glue naming words in the **Nouns** box. Glue action words in the **Verbs** box.

Nouns	Verbs

cut ✂ –

boy

jump

cat

sit

throw

house

swim

fork

193

Words That Describe

Directions: Read the words in the box. Choose the word that describes, or tells about, the picture. Write it next to the picture.

wet	round	funny	soft	sad	tall

_____

_____

_____

_____

_____

_____

Name _____

Words That Describe

Directions: Circle the describing word in each sentence. Draw a line from the sentence to the picture.

1. The hungry dog is eating.

2. The tiny bird is flying.

3. Horses have long legs.

4. She is a fast runner.

5. The little boy was lost.

196

Name _____

Words That Describe: Colors and Numbers

Colors and numbers can describe nouns.

Directions: Underline the describing word in each sentence. Draw a picture to go with each sentence.

A yellow moon was in the sky.

Two worms are on the road.

The tree had red apples.

The girl wore a blue dress.

Name _____

Words That Describe

Describing words tell us more about a person, place, or thing.

Directions: Read the words in the box. Choose a word that describes the picture. Write it next to the picture.

happy	round	sick	cold	long

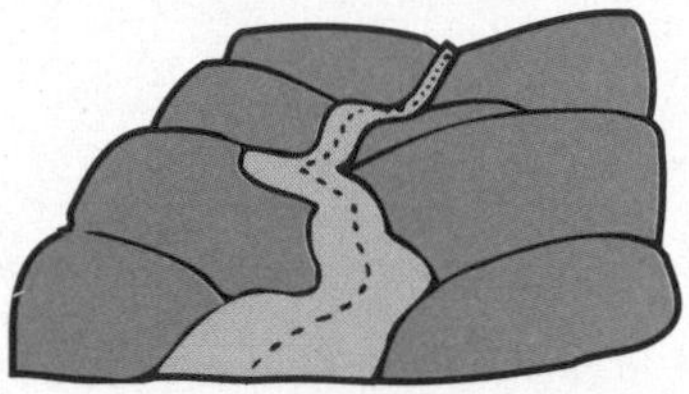

_____

- - - - - - - - - - - - - - - -

_____

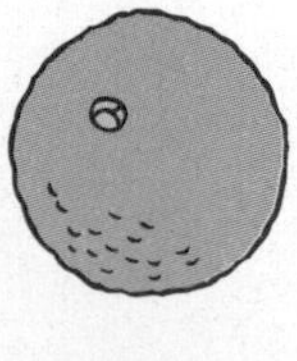

- - - - - - - - - - - - - - - -

_____

- - - - - - - - - - - - - - - -

_____

- - - - - - - - - - - - - - - -

_____

- - - - - - - - - - - - - - - -

_____

Name _____

Adjectives

Describing words are also called **adjectives**.

Directions: Circle the describing words in the sentences.

1. The juicy apple is on the plate.

2. The furry dog is eating a bone.

3. It was a sunny day.

4. The kitten drinks warm milk.

5. The baby has a loud cry.

Name _____

We're the Same!

Words that mean the **same** thing, or close to the same thing, are called **synonyms**.

Directions: Write a word from the word list that has the same meaning as each word below.

Word List			
bright	hop	dad	fast
pretty	plate	silly	center

 **sunny**
_____

 **beautiful**
_____

 **middle**
_____

 **dish**
_____

 **quick**
_____

 **jump**
_____

goofy
_____

 **father**
_____

Name _____

Synonym Squares!

Directions: Circle the **synonym** in each square that has the same meaning or close to the same meaning as the word in **bold** print. The first one is done for you.

end **start**	scream **shout**	cat **sick**
(begin)	brother	bath
stop	talk	ill

Directions: Think of a synonym for each of the three listed words. Then, write a sentence using **both** words in your sentence.

smart/ _____

_____

_____

bad/ _____

_____

_____

little/ _____

_____

_____

Name _____

Take My Place

Directions: Choose the word from the word list below that could take the place of the underlined word in each sentence. Write it on the line.

Word List		
pick	tired	cut
porch	pull	bag

1. I was so <u>sleepy</u>! I couldn't wait to go to
   bed! _____

2. Please put all your books in this <u>sack</u>.

   _____

3. Please <u>choose</u> a present you would like
   to open. _____

4. Are you strong enough to <u>drag</u> this
   heavy crate? _____

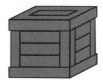

5. "It is important to <u>trim</u> the extra fabric on
   your art project," said my art teacher.

   _____

6. We sipped lemonade on the <u>deck</u>.

   _____

Name _____

Antonym Artists!

Antonyms are words that have **opposite** meanings. Abby and Abe are Antonym Artists! They like to draw opposite pictures.

Directions: Help Abe draw the opposite of Abby's pictures.

Name _____

Oops! It's Opposite Day!

Oppie woke up early one morning to discover it was Opposite Day! Everything was opposite! Oppie got dressed, and all his clothes went on backwards!

Directions: Help Oppie by circling the word in each row that has the **opposite** meaning of the first word.

pull	push	pillow	grab
fast	burger	danger	slow
thin	fat	tall	skinny
break	fix	hold	glue
harm	ham	cold	help
winter	February	summer	fall
loser	bad	teacher	winner

Name _____

Antonyms Are Opposites!

Words with **opposite** meanings are called **antonyms**.

Directions: Circle an antonym for the underlined word in each sentence.

1. The sky was very <u>dark</u>.   purple   old   light

2. Turn <u>left</u> at the light.   right   sideways   yellow

3. The shelf was very <u>high</u>.   pretty   low   loud

4. The turtle walked <u>slowly</u>.   silly   quickly   nicely

5. I <u>whispered</u> at the circus.   laughed   coughed   shouted

6. Bobby is an <u>adult</u>.   child   fan   principal

7. The clown was very <u>strong</u>.   weak   silly   hungry

8. The library is a <u>quiet</u> place.   fun   messy   noisy

Name _____

Batty Bats!

Some words have more than one meaning.

The word **bat** has more than one meaning.

Directions: Look at the words and their meanings below. Next to each picture, write the number that has the correct meaning.

can: 1. a metal container
2. to know how

band: 1. a group of musicians
2. a strip of material

cap: 1. a soft hat with a visor
2. lid or cover

crow: 1. a large black bird
2. the loud cry of a rooster

Name _____

Match That Meaning!

Some words have more than one meaning. Look at the list of words.

Directions: Match the word's correct meaning to the pictures below.

cross: 1. to draw a line through
2. angry

fall: 3. the season between summer and winter
4. to trip or stumble

land: 5. to bring to a stop or rest
6. the ground

_____

_____

_____

_____

_____

_____

Name _____

Match That Meaning!

The word **may** has more than one meaning.

May or   1. the fifth month of the year
may: 2. to be permitted or allowed
               to do something

MAY						
Sunday	Monday	Tuesday	Wednesday	Thursday	Friday	Saturday
			1	2	3	4
5	6	7	8	9	10	11
12	13	14	15	16	17	18
19	20	21	22	23	24	25
26	27	28	29	30	31	

May I please have a drink of water?

Directions: Write the letter of the correct meaning in each blank.

1. My dad's birthday is in _____.

2. _____ I please go to the gym?

3. Many flowers bloom in _____.

4. Mother, _____ I go to the swimming party?

5. My brother will come home from college in _____.

Name _____

Homonyms

Homonyms are words that sound the same, but are spelled differently and have different meanings. For example, **sun** and **son** are homonyms.

Directions: Look at the word. Circle the picture that goes with the word.

1. sun

2. hi

3. ate

4. four

5. buy

6. hear

Name _____

Homonyms

Directions: Look at each picture. Circle the homonym that is spelled the correct way.

deer   dear

blue   blew

to   two

hi   high

by   bye

new   knew

ate   eight

red   read

Name _____

Homonyms

Directions: Write the word from the box that has the same sound but a different meaning next to each picture.

ball	see	blew	pear

bawl   _____

pair   _____

sea   _____

blue   _____

Homonyms

Directions: Jane is having a birthday party. Complete each sentence with a homonym from the box. Then, write the word in the puzzle.

blew	son
blue	two
too	to
sun	write
right	bee
be	knew
new	

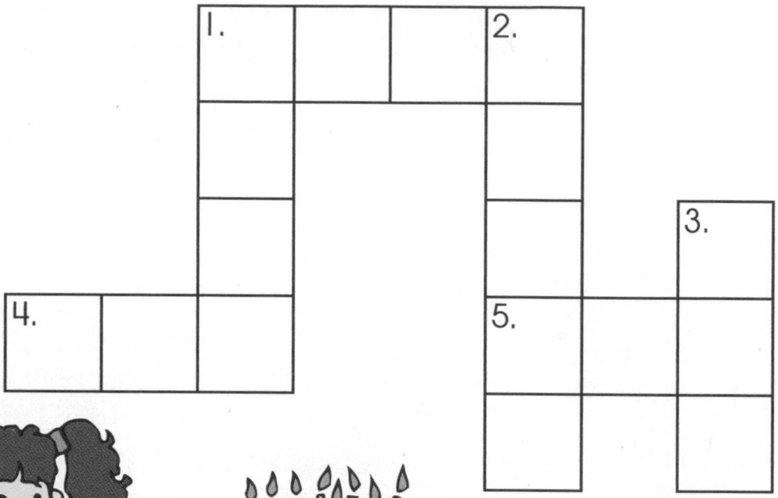

Across:

1. Jane _____ out the candles.

4. Two days ago, she was stung by

   a _____ .

5. But after _____ days, she felt better.

Down:

1. She has on a _____ dress for her party.

2. She will _____ a letter to her grandma.

3. Jane is a girl, so she is not a

   _____ .

Name _____

Make Compound Words

Some short words can be put together to make one new word. The new word is called a **compound word**.

cow + hand = cowhand

Directions: Look at each pair of pictures and words below. Join the two words to make a compound word. Write it on the line.

rain + coat = _____

door + bell = _____

dog + house = _____

pan + cake = _____

horse + shoe = _____

Name _____

Two Words in One

Directions: Write the two words that make up each compound word below.

snowball

_____ _____

raincoat

_____ _____

airplane

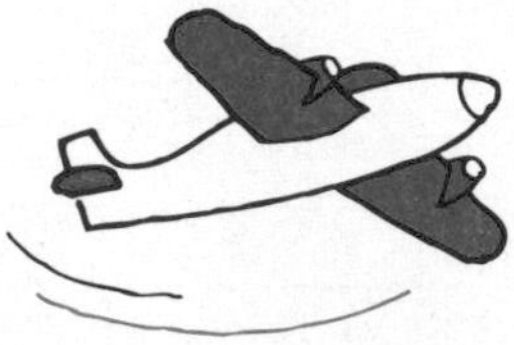

_____ _____

watermelon

_____ _____

haircut

_____ _____

football

_____ _____

sunshine

_____ _____

Name _____

Compound Word Riddles

Directions: Underline the two words in each sentence that can make a compound word. Write the compound word on the line to complete the sentence.

A kind of bird that is black is a
_____
- -
_____.

A horse that can race is a
_____
- -
_____.

A cloth that covers a table is a
_____
- -
_____.

A room with a bed is a
_____
- -
_____.

A book with a story is a
_____
- -
_____.

A bowl that holds fish is a
_____
- -
_____.

Name _____

Compound Words

Directions: Look at the pictures and the two words that are next to each other. Put the words together to make a new word. Write the new word.

Example:

house + boat =

houseboat

side + walk =

_____

lip + stick =

_____

sand + box =

_____

lunch + box =

_____

Name _____

Compound Words

Directions: Cut out the pictures and words at the bottom of the page. Put two words together to make a compound word. Write the new word.

[ ] + [ ] = _____

[ ] + [ ] = _____

[ ] + [ ] = _____

[ ] + [ ] = _____

cut ✂ -

mail | snow | ball | bow

basket | man | rain | box

Name _____

Compound Words

Directions: Circle the compound word that completes each sentence.
Write each word on the lines.

_____
- - - - - - - - - - - - - - - - - -

1. The _____ brings us letters.
   mailman   snowman

_____
- - - - - - - - - - - - - - - - - -

2. A _____ grows tall.
   sunlight   sunflower

_____
- - - - - - - - - - - - - - - - - -

3. The snow falls _____ .
   outside   inside

_____
- - - - - - - - - - - - - - - - - -

4. A _____ fell on my head.
   raindrop   rainbow

_____
- - - - - - - - - - - - - - - - - -

5. I put the letter in a _____ .
   mailbox   shoebox

Name _____

Compound Words

Directions: Draw lines to make compound words. Write the new words on the lines.

Example: song + bird = songbird.

dog   room

foot   box

bed   house

mail   light

some   ball

moon   thing

_____   _____

_____   _____

_____   _____

Compound Words

Directions: Read the sentences. Fill in the blank with a compound word from the word box.

| raincoat | bedroom | lunchbox | hallway | sandbox |

1. A box with sand is a

_____ .

2. The way through a hall is a

_____ .

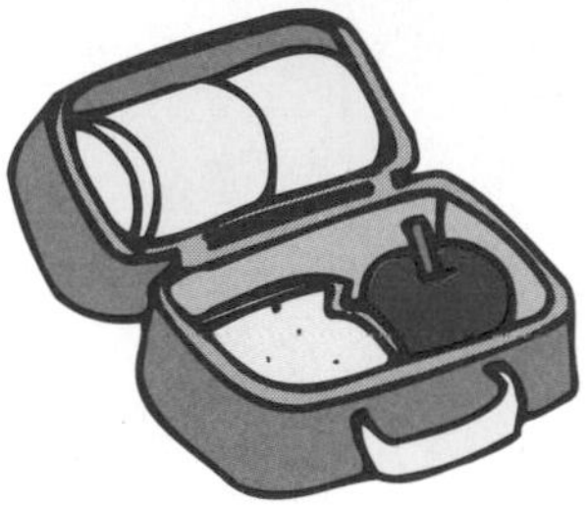

3. A box for lunch is a

_____ .

4. A coat for the rain is a

_____ .

5. A room with a bed is a

_____ .

One or More Than One?

Directions: Circle the correct word under each picture. The first one is done for you.

hat   (hats)   car   cars   frog   frogs

shirt   shirts   cloud   clouds   wheel   wheels

dish   dishes   glass   glasses   fox   foxes

Name _____

How Many Toys?

Directions: Read the nouns under the pictures. Write each noun under **One** or **More Than One**.

 yo-yos

 jet

 doll

 blocks

boat

cars

 drum

 balls

One	**More Than One**

Making Nouns Plural

A **plural noun** means more than one. Add **s** to most nouns to make plural nouns.

Example: Penny has one **dog**.
Jerry has two **dogs**.

Directions: Write the plural form of the nouns below.

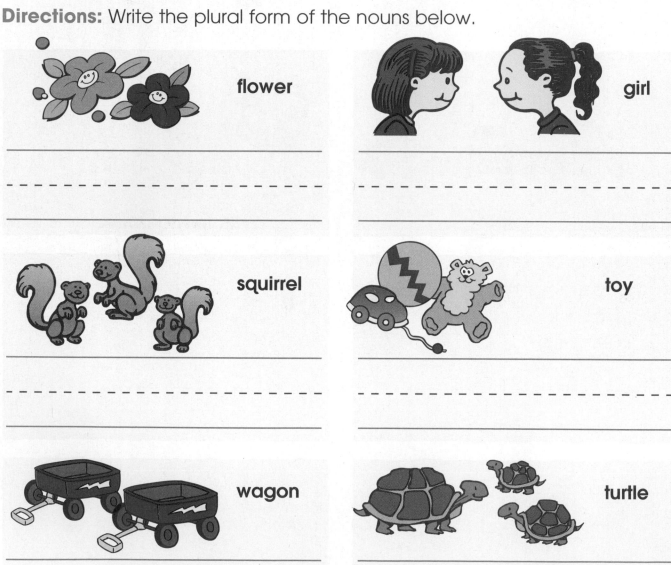

flower

_____

- - - - - - - - - - - - - - -

_____

girl

_____

- - - - - - - - - - - - - - -

_____

squirrel

_____

- - - - - - - - - - - - - - -

_____

toy

_____

- - - - - - - - - - - - - - -

_____

wagon

_____

- - - - - - - - - - - - - - -

_____

turtle

_____

- - - - - - - - - - - - - - -

_____

Name _____

More Than One

Some nouns name more than one person, place, or thing.

Directions: Add **s** to make the words tell about the picture.

frog____

pan____

boy____

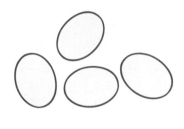

egg____

horn____

girl____

Name _____

More Than One

An **s** at the end of a word often means there is more than one. Words that mean more than one are also called **plurals**.

Directions: Look at each picture and circle the correct word. Write the word on the line.

two

dog   dogs

_____

— — — — — — —

_____

four

flower   flowers

_____

— — — — — — —

_____

one

bikes   bike

_____

— — — — — — —

_____

three

toys   toy

_____

— — — — — — —

_____

a

lamb   lambs

_____

— — — — — — —

_____

two

cat   cats

_____

— — — — — — —

_____

Name _____

One Is Not Enough!

A plural noun means more than one. To make nouns that end in **x**, **s**, **ss**, **sh**, or **ch** plural, add **es**.

Example: Barry filled one **box** with sand.
Barry filled four **boxes** with sand.

Directions: Write the plural form of each noun below.

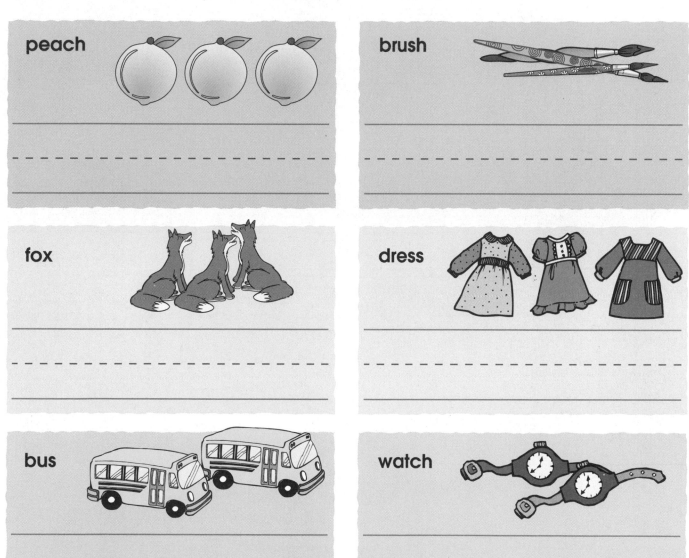

peach

brush

fox

dress

bus

watch

Name _____

Use the Clues

Directions: Write each word from the word box in the correct place. Remember that plural forms usually end in **s**.

kites	star	chick	foxes	matches	lunch

One

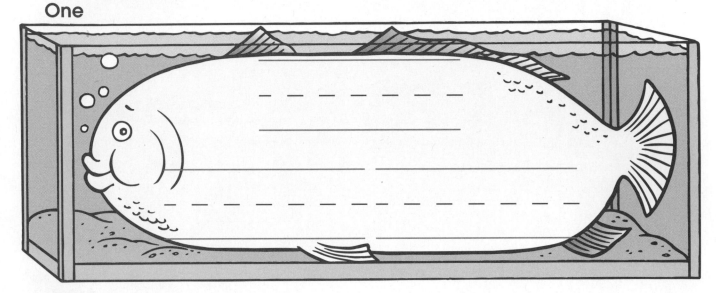

More Than One (Plural)

228

Name _____

Sentences That Tell

Some sentences tell something. Every **telling sentence** ends with a **period**.

Example: The bird sings.

Directions: Circle only the sentences that tell something.

1. Two turtles sat on a log.

2. One turtle fell off.

3. Did you see her?

4. She swam away.

5. The water is cold.

6. Can you swim?

Sentences

Sentences begin with capital letters.

Directions: Read the sentences and write them below. Begin each sentence with a capital letter.

Example: the cat is fat.

my dog is big.

_____

_ _ _ _ _ _ _ _ _ _ _ _ _ _ _ _

_____

the boy is sad.

_____

_ _ _ _ _ _ _ _ _ _ _ _ _ _ _ _

_____

bikes are fun!

_____

_ _ _ _ _ _ _ _ _ _ _ _ _ _ _ _

_____

dad can bake.

_____

_ _ _ _ _ _ _ _ _ _ _ _ _ _ _ _

_____

Name _____

Statements

A **statement** is a sentence that tells something. It begins with a capital letter and ends with a period. **Example:** The Moon orbits the Earth.

Directions: If the sentence is a statement, color the space black. If it is not, color the space yellow.

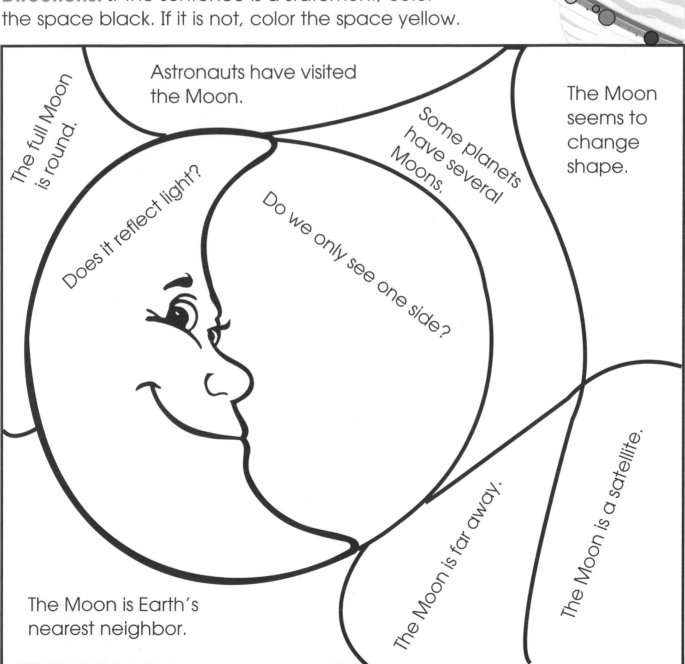

The full Moon is round.

Astronauts have visited the Moon.

The Moon seems to change shape.

Some planets have several Moons.

Does it reflect light?

Do we only see one side?

The Moon is Earth's nearest neighbor.

The Moon is far away.

The Moon is a satellite.

Name _____

Writing Sentences

A **sentence** begins with a capital letter and ends with a period.

Directions: Read the two sentences on each line. Draw a line between the two sentences. Then, write each sentence correctly.

i have a new bike   it is red

_____

_____

_____

we are twins   we look just alike

_____

_____

_____

the baby is crying   she wants a bottle

_____

_____

_____

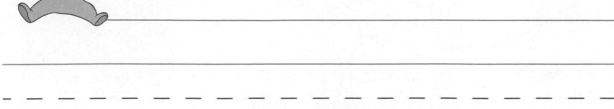

Name _____

Making Sentences

A **sentence** tells a whole idea.

Directions: Cut out and glue each picture and group of words together to make a sentence.

233

Sentence Building

Sentences can tell a story.

Directions: Read each sentence. Cut out and glue the sentence that tells what happened next. Write a sentence that tells what could happen after that.

Mary went to bed and quickly fell asleep.

Glue

Brad saw something shiny in the grass.

Glue

Sally wanted a pet for her birthday.

Glue

He bent down to see what it was.

Her mom took her to the pet store.

She began to have an amazing dream.

Completing Sentences

A **sentence** must make sense.

Directions: Match each sentence with an ending which makes sense. Circle the correct ending.

the first day of school.

1. Today is

on the window.

around the corner.

2. I like to

walk to school with my friend.

at noon every day.

3. We eat lunch

on the roof.

under the old tree.

4. My class

is learning to read.

pencil on my desk.

5. I put my

in the small box.

three more times.

6. Our classroom

has a map on the wall.

Name _____

Subjects of Sentences

The **subject** of a sentence tells who or what does something.

Examples: Polar bears love cold weather.
The bear's coat is thick.

Directions: Circle the subject of each sentence.

1. Polar bears live in the Arctic.

2. The Arctic is very cold.

3. The polar bear's coat is white.

4. The fur coat keeps the bear warm.

5. The bear has a layer of fat under its skin.

6. The fat is called *blubber*.

7. Blubber keeps the bear warm, too.

8. Polar bears eat seals.

9. A polar bear can sneak up on a seal.

10. The bear's white coat makes it hard to see.

Name _____

Predicates of Sentences

The **predicate** of a sentence tells what the subject is or does.

Examples: Parrots **are not all alike**.
Some parrots **can learn tricks**.

Directions: Circle the predicate of each sentence.

1. Parrots live in hot places.

2. Some macaws are three-feet long.

3. Macaws live in rainforests.

4. Other parrots build nests in desert cactuses.

5. Most parrots have long beaks.

6. They use their beaks for cracking nuts.

7. Some parrots cannot crack nuts.

8. They eat seeds and fruits instead.

9. Parrots are colorful birds.

10. These birds have loud voices.

Name _____

Questions

A **question** is a sentence that asks something. It begins with a capital letter and ends with a question mark.

Example: Have you ever visited a farm? What animals lived on the farm?

Directions: If the sentence is a question, put a **question mark** at the end and color the barn red. If it is not, draw an **X** on the barn.

1. I'm going to visit my grandma

2. Would you like to go with me

3. Will you ask your mother

4. Did she say you could go

5. What would you like to do first

6. Do you want to see the ducks

7. There are four of them on the pond

8. We'll see the baby chicks next

9. Are you glad you came with me

10. Maybe you can come again

Name _____

More Questions

Directions: A **question** begins with a capital letter and ends with a question mark. Look at each picture of Panda. Ask Panda a question to go with each picture.

_____

_____

_____

_____

_____

_____

Changing Sentences

The order of words can change a sentence.

Directions: Read each telling sentence. Change the order of the words to make an asking sentence. **Example:**

The clown is happy.

Is the clown happy?

The boy can swim.

The bell will ring.

The popcorn is hot.

The flowers are lovely.

Name _____

Sentences That Ask

Some sentences ask something. An **asking sentence** is called a **question**. A question ends with a **question mark**.

Example: What is your name?

Directions: Circle only the questions.

1. Is that your house?

2. There are two pictures on the wall.

3. Where do you sleep?

4. Do you watch TV in that room?

5. Which coat is yours?

6. The kitten is asleep.

Name _____

Questions, Questions

A **question** begins with a capital letter and ends with a question mark.

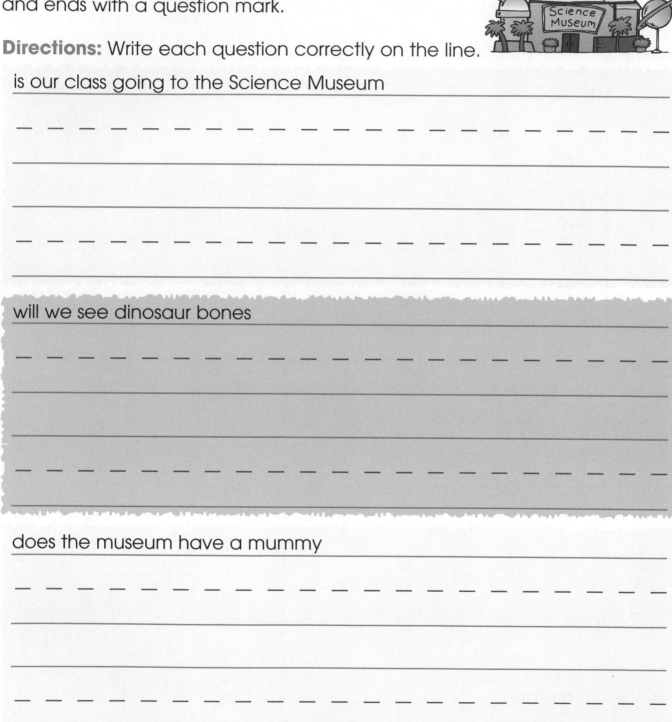

Directions: Write each question correctly on the line.

is our class going to the Science Museum

_ _

_____

_ _

_____

will we see dinosaur bones

_ _

_____

_ _

_____

does the museum have a mummy

_ _

_____

_____

_____

I'm So Excited!

The end mark **!** shows that you are excited.
Use it to end a sentence that shows strong feelings.

Example: What a beautiful day this is**!**

Directions: Read these sentences. Write **?** or **!** after each sentence.

? or !

1. What a great day this is for a race ☐

2. Who is running in this race ☐

3. How fast they run ☐

4. Who will finish first ☐

5. The runners are off ☐

6. Run faster ☐

7. Can you see the finish line ☐

8. I won the race ☐

Surprising Sequence

Some sentences show a strong feeling and end with an **exclamation mark** (**!**). A surprising sentence may be only one or two words showing fear, surprise, or pain, such as "Oh, no!"

Directions: Put a **period** at the end of the sentences that tell something. Put an **exclamation mark** at the end of the sentences that show a strong feeling. Put a **question mark** at the end of the sentences that ask a question.

1. The cheetah can run very fast

2. Wow

3. Look at that cheetah go

4. Can you run fast

5. Oh, my

6. You're faster than I am

7. Let's run together

8. We can run as fast as a cheetah

9. What fun

10. Do you think cheetahs get tired

Sentence Sequence

The words in a sentence must be in the correct order.

Directions: Cut out and glue the words in the correct order to tell about each picture.

1.

2.

3.

1.	2.	3.
is going	We are taking	to swim
to the beach.	of food.	It's fun
My family	a basket	in the ocean.

Name _____

Word Order

Word order is the order of words in a sentence which makes sense.

Directions: Cut out the words and put them in the correct order. Glue each sentence on another sheet of paper.

| I | like | bike. | to | ride | my |

| hot. | It | is | and | sunny |

| drink | I | can | water. |

| My | me. | with | plays | mom |

| tricks. | do | can | The | dog |

| you | go | store? | to | the | Can |

Name _____

ABC Order

Sometimes, words are put in **ABC order**. That means that if a word starts with **a**, it comes first. If it starts with **b**, it comes next, and so on in the order of the alphabet.

Directions: Circle the first letter of each word below. Then, put the words in ABC order. The first one is done for you.

Ⓒar   Ⓑird   moon   two   nest   fan

bird _____   _____

car _____   _____

card   dog   pig   bike   sun   pie

_____   _____   _____

_____   _____   _____

ABC Order

Directions: Put each row of words in ABC order. If the first letters of two words are the same, look at the second or third letters.

Example:

1. __1__ candy   __2__ carrot   __4__ duck   __3__ dance

2. _____ cold   _____ hot   _____ carry   _____ hit

3. _____ flash   _____ fan   _____ fun   _____ garden

4. _____ seat   _____ sun   _____ saw   _____ sit

5. _____ row   _____ ring   _____ rock   _____ run

6. _____ truck   _____ turn   _____ twin   _____ talk

7. _____ seven   _____ shoe   _____ soap   _____ smell

8. _____ pay   _____ penny   _____ pocket   _____ plant

Test Practice Table of Contents

About the Tests

What Are Standardized Achievement Tests?

Achievement tests measure what children know in particular subject areas such as reading, language arts, and mathematics. They do not measure your child's intelligence or ability to learn.

When tests are standardized, or *normed*, children's test results are compared with those of a specific group who have taken the test, usually at the same age or grade.

Standardized achievement tests measure what children around the country are learning. The test makers survey popular textbook series, as well as state curriculum frameworks and other professional sources, to determine what content is covered widely.

Because of variations in state frameworks and textbook series, as well as grade ranges on some test levels, the tests may cover some material that children have not yet learned. This is especially true if the test is offered early in the school year. However, test scores are compared to those of other children who take the test at the same time of year, so your child will not be at a disadvantage if his or her class has not covered specific material yet.

Different School Districts, Different Tests

There are many flexible options for districts when offering standardized tests. Many school districts choose not to give the full test battery, but select certain content and scoring options. For example, many schools may test only in the areas of reading and mathematics. Similarly, a state or district may use one test for certain grades and another test for other grades. These decisions are often based on

the amount of time and money a district wishes to spend on test administration. Some states choose to develop their own statewide assessment tests.

On pages 255–257 you will find information about these five widely used standardized achievement tests:

- California Achievement Test (CAT)
- Terra Nova/CTBS
- Iowa Test of Basic Skills (ITBS)
- Stanford Achievement Test (SAT9)
- Metropolitan Achievement Test (MAT)

However, this book contains strategies and practice questions for use with a variety of tests. Even if your state does not give one of the five tests listed above, your child will benefit from doing the practice questions in this book. If you're unsure about which test your child takes, contact your local school district to find out which tests are given.

Types of Test Questions

Traditionally, standardized achievement tests have used only multiple-choice questions. Today, many tests may include constructed response (short answer) and extended response (essay) questions as well.

In addition, many tests include questions that tap students' higher-order thinking skills. Instead of simple recall questions, such as identifying a date in history, questions may require students to make comparisons and contrasts or analyze results, among other skills.

What the Tests Measure

These tests do not measure your child's level of intelligence, but they do show how well your child knows material that he or she has learned and that is

also covered on the tests. It's important to remember that some tests cover content that is not taught in your child's school or grade. In other instances, depending on when in the year the test is given, your child may not yet have covered the material.

If the test reports you receive show that your child needs improvement in one or more skill areas, you may want to seek help from your child's teacher and find out how you can work with your child to improve his or her skills.

California Achievement Test (CAT/5)

What Is the California Achievement Test?

The *California Achievement Test* is a standardized achievement test battery that is widely used with elementary through high school students.

Parts of the Test

The *CAT* includes tests in the following content areas:

Reading
- Word Analysis
- Vocabulary
- Comprehension

Spelling

Language Arts
- Language Mechanics
- Language Usage

Mathematics

Science

Social Studies

Your child may take some or all of these subtests if your district uses the *California Achievement Test*.

Terra Nova/CTBS (Comprehensive Tests of Basic Skills)

What Is the Terra Nova/CTBS?

The *Terra Nova/Comprehensive Tests of Basic Skills* is a standardized achievement test battery used in elementary through high school grades.

While many of the test questions on the Terra Nova are in the traditional multiple choice form, your child may take parts of the Terra Nova that include some open-ended questions (constructed-response items).

Parts of the Test

Your child may take some or all of the following subtests if your district uses the *Terra Nova/CTBS*:

Reading/Language Arts

Mathematics

Science

Social Studies

Supplementary tests include:
- Word Analysis
- Vocabulary
- Language Mechanics
- Spelling
- Mathematics Computation

Critical thinking skills may also be tested.

Iowa Test of Basic Skills (ITBS)

What Is the ITBS?

The *Iowa Test of Basic Skills* is a standardized achievement test battery used in elementary through high school grades.

Parts of the Test

Your child may take some or all of these subtests if your district uses the *ITBS*, also known as the *Iowa*:

Reading
- Vocabulary
- Reading Comprehension

Language Arts
- Spelling
- Capitalization
- Punctuation
- Usage and Expression

Math
- Concepts/Estimate
- Problems/Data Interpretation

Social Studies

Science

Sources of Information

Stanford Achievement Test (SAT9)

What Is the Stanford Achievement Test?

The *Stanford Achievement Test, Ninth Edition (SAT9)* is a standardized achievement test battery used in elementary through high school grades.

Note that the *Stanford Achievement Test (SAT9)* is a different test from the *SAT* used by high school students for college admissions.

While many of the test questions on the *SAT9* are in traditional multiple choice form, your child may take parts of the *SAT9* that include some open-ended questions (constructed-response items).

Parts of the Test

Your child may take some or all of these subtests if your district uses the *Stanford Achievement Test*:

Reading
- Vocabulary
- Reading Comprehension

Mathematics
- Problem Solving
- Procedures

Language Arts

Spelling

Study Skills

Listening
Critical thinking skills may also be tested.

Metropolitan Achievement Test (MAT7 and MAT8)

What Is the Metropolitan Achievement Test?

The *Metropolitan Achievement Test* is a standardized achievement test battery used in elementary through high school grades.

Parts of the Test

Your child may take some or all of these subtests if your district uses the *Metropolitan Achievement Test*:

Reading
- Vocabulary
- Reading Comprehension

Math
- Concepts and Problem Solving
- Computation

Language Arts
- Pre-writing
- Composing
- Editing

Science

Social Studies

Research Skills

Thinking Skills

Spelling

Statewide Assessments

Today, the majority of states give statewide assessments. In some cases, these tests are known as *high-stakes assessments*. This means that students must score at a certain level in order to be promoted. Some states use minimum competency or proficiency tests. Often, these tests measure more basic skills than other types of statewide assessments.

Statewide assessments are generally linked to state curriculum frameworks. Frameworks provide a blueprint, or outline, to ensure that teachers are covering the same curriculum topics as other teachers in the same grade level in the state. In some states, standardized achievement tests (such as the five described in this book) are used in connection with statewide assessments.

When Statewide Assessments Are Given

Statewide assessments may not be given at every grade level. Generally, they are offered at one or more grades in elementary school, middle school, and high school. Many states test at grades 4, 8, and 10.

State-by-State Information

You can find information about statewide assessments and curriculum frameworks at your state Department of Education Web site. To find the address for your individual state, go to www.ed.gov, click on Topics A–Z, and then click on State Departments of Education. You will find a list of all the state departments of education, mailing addresses, and Web sites.

How to Help Your Child Prepare for Standardized Testing

Preparing All Year Round

Perhaps the most valuable way you can help your child prepare for standardized achievement tests is by providing enriching experiences. Keep in mind also that test results for younger children are not as reliable as for older students. If a child is hungry, tired, or upset, this may result in a poor test score. Here are some tips on how you can help your child do his or her best on standardized tests.

Read aloud with your child. Reading aloud helps develop vocabulary and fosters a positive attitude toward reading. Reading together is one of the most effective ways you can help your child succeed in school.

Share experiences. Baking cookies together, planting a garden, or making a map of your neighborhood are examples of activities that help build skills that are measured on the tests, such as sequencing and following directions.

Become informed about your state's testing procedures. Ask about or watch for announcements of meetings that explain about standardized tests and statewide assessments in your school district. Talk to your child's teacher about your child's individual performance on these state tests during a parent-teacher conference.

Help your child know what to expect. Read and discuss with your child the test-taking tips in this book. Your child can prepare by working through a couple of strategies a day so that no practice session takes too long.

Help your child with his or her regular school assignments. Set up a quiet study area for homework. Supply this area with pencils, paper, markers, a calculator, a ruler, a dictionary, scissors, glue, and so on. Check your child's homework and offer to help if he or she gets stuck. But remember, it's your child's homework, not yours. If you help too much, your child will not benefit from the activity.

Keep in regular contact with your child's teacher. Attend parent-teacher conferences, school functions, PTA or PTO meetings, and school board meetings. This will help you get to know the educators in your district and the families of your child's classmates.

Learn to use computers as an educational resource. If you do not have a computer and Internet access at home, try your local library.

Remember—simply getting your child comfortable with testing procedures and helping him or her know what to expect can improve test scores!

Getting Ready for the Big Day

There are lots of things you can do on or immediately before test day to improve your child's chances of testing success. What's more, these strategies will help your child prepare him- or herself for school tests, too, and promote general study skills that can last a lifetime.

Provide a good breakfast on test day.
Instead of sugar cereal, which provides immediate but not long-term energy, have your child eat a breakfast with protein or complex carbohydrates, such as an egg, whole grain cereal or toast, or a banana-yogurt shake.

Assure your child that he or she is not expected to know all of the answers on the test. Explain that other children in higher grades may take the same test, and that the test may measure things your child has not yet learned in school. Help your child understand that you expect him or her to put forth a good effort—and that this is enough. Your child should not try to cram for these tests. Also avoid threats or bribes; these put undue pressure on children and may interfere with their best performance.

Promote a good night's sleep. A good night's sleep before the test is essential. Try not to overstress the importance of the test. This may cause your child to lose sleep because of anxiety. Doing some exercise after school and having a quiet evening routine will help your child sleep well the night before the test.

Keep the mood light and offer encouragement. To provide a break on test days, do something fun and special after school—take a walk around the neighborhood, play a game, read a favorite book, or prepare a special snack together. These activities keep your child's mood light—even if the testing sessions have been difficult—and show how much you appreciate your child's effort.

Taking Standardized Tests

What You Need to Know About Taking Tests

You can get better at taking tests. Here are some tips.

Do your schoolwork. Study in school. Do your homework all the time. These things will help you in school and on any tests you take. Learn new things a little at a time. Then, you will remember them better when you see them on a test.

Feel your best. One way you can do your best on tests and in school is to make sure your body is ready. Get a good night's sleep. Eat a healthy breakfast.

One more thing: Wear comfortable clothes. You can also wear your lucky shirt or your favorite color on test day. It can't hurt. It may even make you feel better about the test.

Be ready for the test. Do practice questions. Learn about the different kinds of questions. Books like this one will help you.

Follow the test directions. Listen carefully to the directions your teacher gives. Read all instructions carefully. Watch out for words such as *not*, *none*, *never*, *all*, and *always*. These words can change the meaning of the directions. You may want to circle words like these. This will help you keep them in mind as you answer the questions.

Look carefully at each page before you start. Do reading tests in a special order. First, read the directions. Read the questions next. This way you will know what to look for as you read. Then, read the story. Last, read the story again quickly. Skim it to find the best answer.

On math tests, look at the labels on graphs and charts. Think about what the graph or chart shows. You will often need to draw conclusions about the information to answer some questions.

Use your time wisely. Many tests have time limits. Look at the clock when the test starts. Figure out when you need to stop. When you begin, look over the whole thing. Do the easy parts first. Go back and do the hard parts last. Make sure you do not spend too much time on any one part. This way, if you run out of time, you still have completed much of the test.

Fill in the answer circles the right way. Fill in the whole circle. Make your pencil mark dark, but not so dark that it goes through the paper! Be sure you pick just one answer for each question. If you pick two answers, both will be marked as wrong.

Use context clues to figure out hard questions. You may come across a word or an idea you don't understand. First, try to say it in your own words. Then use context clues—the words in the sentences nearby—to help you figure out its meaning.

Sometimes it's good to guess. Here's what to do. Each question may have four or five answer choices. You may know that two answers are wrong, but you are not sure about the rest. Then make your best guess. If you are not sure about any of the answers, skip it. Do not guess. Tests like these take away extra points for wrong answers. So it is better to leave them blank.

Check your work. You may finish the test before the time is up. Then, you can go back and check your answers. Make sure you answered each question you could. Also, make sure that you filled in only one answer circle for each question. Erase any extra marks on the page.

Finally—stay calm! Take time to relax before the test. One good way to relax is to get some exercise. Stretch, shake out your fingers, and wiggle your toes. Take a few slow, deep breaths. Then picture yourself doing a great job!

Name _____

READING: WORD ANALYSIS

● **Lesson 1: Letter Recognition**

Directions: Look at the word your teacher reads. Mark the letter the word begins with. Example A is done for you. Practice with example B.

Examples

A. Which letter does the word **sand** begin with?
- (A) b
- (B) l
- (C) s
- (D) c

B. Which letter does the word **large** begin with?
- (F) p
- (G) q
- (H) m
- (J) l

If you are not sure which answer is correct, take your best guess. Eliminate answer choices you know are wrong.

● **Practice**

1. Which letter does the word **park** begin with?
- (A) v
- (B) w
- (C) b
- (D) p

2. Which letter does the word **dog** begin with?
- (F) d
- (G) b
- (H) y
- (J) o

3. Which letter does the word **nice** begin with?
- (A) s
- (B) n
- (C) u
- (D) k

4. Which letter does the word **talk** begin with?
- (F) j
- (G) f
- (H) t
- (J) l

STOP

Name _____

READING: WORD ANALYSIS

● **Lesson 2: Beginning Sounds**

Directions: Look at the picture. Listen to your teacher read the word. Listen to your teacher read the words to the right of the picture. Mark the word with the same beginning sound as the picture. Practice with example A.

Example

A. desk

- (A) chair
- (B) den
- (C) bat
- (D) man

 Clue Say the name of the picture to yourself. Listen closely to the word choices.

● **Practice**

1. rabbit

- (A) man
- (B) bike
- (C) paper
- (D) ring

3. bag

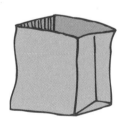

- (A) vase
- (B) top
- (C) bell
- (D) fish

2. mop

- (F) miss
- (G) hill
- (H) clock
- (J) win

4. tie

- (F) tag
- (G) girl
- (H) shell
- (J) pin   STOP

READING: WORD ANALYSIS

● **Lesson 3: Ending Sounds**

Directions: Listen to your teacher read all the words. Mark the word with the same ending sound as the first word. Practice with examples A and B.

Examples

A. make

- (A) cat
- (B) rock
- (C) worm
- (D) pen

B. hive

- (F) web
- (G) fun
- (H) glove
- (J) tip

 Clue Listen carefully to the ending sound of each word.

● **Practice**

1. star

- (A) mop
- (B) leaf
- (C) jar
- (D) five

2. leg

- (F) rug
- (G) gone
- (H) rich
- (J) grab

3. stew

- (A) net
- (B) wheel
- (C) barn
- (D) now

4. hit

- (F) dish
- (G) win
- (H) not
- (J) hear

5. bell

- (A) rest
- (B) hill
- (C) boat
- (D) cab

 STOP

Name _____

READING: WORD ANALYSIS

● Lesson 4: Rhyming Words

Directions: Listen to your teacher read the word. Choose the picture that rhymes with the word. Practice with example A.

Example

A. mop

Ⓐ   Ⓑ   Ⓒ

Clue   Look at the pictures. Say the words to yourself. Listen for the ending sound.

● Practice

1. dog

Ⓐ   Ⓑ   Ⓒ

2. hat

Ⓕ   Ⓖ   Ⓗ

3. rock

Ⓐ   Ⓑ   Ⓒ   STOP

Name _____

READING: WORD ANALYSIS

● **Lesson 5: Word Recognition**

Directions: Listen to your teacher read the word. Notice the underlined part. Then, listen as your teacher reads the word choices. Listen for the word with the same sound as the underlined part and mark it. Practice with examples A and B.

Examples

A. mud

- Ⓐ but
- Ⓑ sock
- Ⓒ shell
- Ⓓ cat

B. pound

- Ⓕ snow
- Ⓖ spent
- Ⓗ loud
- Ⓙ rider

 Clue Do numbers 1–4 the same way. You may ask your teacher to repeat an item after all of the word choices have been read one time.

● **Practice**

1. **rose**

- Ⓐ rule
- Ⓑ bake
- Ⓒ pony
- Ⓓ nine

3. **peach**

- Ⓐ quiet
- Ⓑ push
- Ⓒ last
- Ⓓ need

2. **spoon**

- Ⓕ here
- Ⓖ smooth
- Ⓗ after
- Ⓙ chip

4. **ride**

- Ⓕ miss
- Ⓖ line
- Ⓗ street
- Ⓙ horse

 STOP

Name _____

READING: WORD ANALYSIS

● **Lesson 6: Vowel Sounds and Sight Words**

Directions: Listen as your teacher reads the question and says the name of the picture. Then, listen as your teacher reads the word choices. Choose the best answer. Example A is done for you. Practice with example B.

Examples

A. **What word has the same vowel sound as the picture?**

(A) pen
(B) spoon
(C) kite
(D) chip

B. **What word rhymes with shell?**

(F) smell
(G) dog
(H) rode
(J) mile

 Clue Listen to all choices before you mark your answer.

● **Practice**

1. **What word has the same vowel sound as the picture?**

(A) mouse
(B) long
(C) tick
(D) spoon

2. **What word has the same vowel sound as the picture?**

(F) bead
(G) hive
(H) quilt
(J) apple

3. **What word has the same vowel sound as might?**

(A) pin
(B) time
(C) from
(D) soul

4. **What word rhymes with tough?**

(F) crow
(G) pool
(H) puff
(J) ton

Name _____

READING: WORD ANALYSIS

● **Lesson 7: Word Study**

Directions: Listen as your teacher reads the word choices. Mark the word that is a compound word. Practice with example A.

Directions: Listen as your teacher reads the sentence and the word choices. One will fill in the blank. Mark your choice. Practice with example B.

Examples

A.
- Ⓐ airplane
- Ⓑ ringer
- Ⓒ tune

B. The dog _____ its food.
- Ⓕ eat
- Ⓖ ate
- Ⓗ eating

Clue Listen carefully each time your teacher reads directions. The directions may change.

● **Practice**

1.
- Ⓐ toolbox
- Ⓑ kitchen
- Ⓒ gate

2.
- Ⓕ warning
- Ⓖ flowerpot
- Ⓗ glasses

3.
- Ⓐ teacup
- Ⓑ pencil
- Ⓒ jumping

4. **I am _____ than you.**
- Ⓕ big
- Ⓖ bigger
- Ⓗ biggest

5. **I _____ books.**
- Ⓐ readed
- Ⓑ reads
- Ⓒ read

6. **He _____ hot.**
- Ⓕ weren't
- Ⓖ wasn't
- Ⓗ won't

STOP

Name _____

READING: WORD ANALYSIS
SAMPLE TEST

● **Directions:** Listen as your teacher reads the problems and answer choices. Mark the best answer. Practice with example A.

Example

A. **What picture begins with the same sound as nut?**

Ⓐ   Ⓑ   Ⓒ

I. **What picture begins with the same sound as cat?**

Ⓐ   Ⓑ   Ⓒ

2. **What word begins with the same sound as the picture?**

- Ⓕ bat
- Ⓖ pig
- Ⓗ kite
- Ⓙ sun

3. **What letters show the beginning sound of the picture?**

- Ⓐ gl
- Ⓑ tr
- Ⓒ gr
- Ⓓ sl

4. **What word ends with the same sound as get?**

- Ⓕ tip
- Ⓖ sat
- Ⓗ run
- Ⓙ girl

5. **What word ends with the same sound as rash?**

- Ⓐ with
- Ⓑ luck
- Ⓒ push
- Ⓓ itch

GO ON

Name _____

READING: WORD ANALYSIS
SAMPLE TEST (cont.)

● **Directions:** Listen as your teacher reads the words and answer choices. Look at the underlined part. Which word has the same sound as the underlined part? Practice with examples B and C.

Examples

B. rain
- F time
- G tan
- H name
- J spun

C. pie
- A bake
- B pin
- C cup
- D ride

6. pin
- F tip
- G had
- H shut
- J peel

7. mail
- A cat
- B trade
- C kit
- D push

8. sat
- F miss
- G pit
- H ban
- J same

9. spoon
- A touch
- B pool
- C tot
- D pad

10. meet
- F tick
- G piece
- H bun
- J stem

11. haunt
- A paw
- B hat
- C hunt
- D stir

GO ON

READING: WORD ANALYSIS
SAMPLE TEST (cont.)

● **Directions:** Listen as your teacher reads the words. Take away the first letter sound. Replace it with another sound. Mark the picture of the new word it makes.

12. bun

(F)

(G)

(H)

13. tail

(A)

(B)

(C)

● **Directions:** Choose the beginning sound that will make the word shown next to the picture.

14. ___ill

(F) m
(G) h
(H) p

16. ___ant

(F) pl
(G) st
(H) pr

15. ___ell

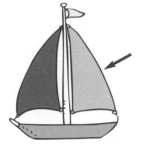

(A) ch
(B) th
(C) sh

STOP

Name _____

READING: VOCABULARY

● **Lesson 8: Picture Vocabulary**

Directions: Listen to your teacher read the sentence. Choose the picture that finishes the sentence. Practice with example A.

Example

A. Bill drinks _____ .

(A)

(B) MILK

(C)

Clue Listen carefully. Think about what you hear while you look at each picture.

● **Practice**

1. I like to read a _____ .

(A)

(B)

(C)

2. The _____ ran fast.

(F)

(G)

(H)

3. The baby _____ in her bed.

(A)

(B)

(C)

4. The _____ rings.

(F)

(G)

(H)

 STOP

Name _____

READING: VOCABULARY

● **Lesson 9: Word Reading**

Directions: Look at the picture. Listen as your teacher reads the word choices. Mark the word that matches the picture. Practice with examples A and B.

Examples

A.
- (A) cat
- (B) flower
- (C) bird

B.
- (F) sing
- (G) bark
- (H) read

 Clue Listen to all answer choices before you choose.

● **Practice**

1.
- (A) mom
- (B) dog
- (C) book

2.
- (F) hug
- (G) cry
- (H) run

3.
- (A) sit
- (B) love
- (C) eat

4.
- (F) land
- (G) shelf
- (H) water

5.
- (A) run
- (B) skip
- (C) swim

6.
- (F) skin
- (G) scales
- (H) cloth

 STOP

Name _____

READING: VOCABULARY

● **Lesson 10: Word Meaning**

Directions: Listen to your teacher read each phrase and the word choices. Mark the word that matches the phrase. Practice with examples A and B.

Examples

A.   to move fast...

- Ⓐ crawl
- Ⓑ run
- Ⓒ walk
- Ⓓ sit

B.   a cold thing...

- Ⓕ ice
- Ⓖ fire
- Ⓗ sun
- Ⓙ stove

 Clue   Be sure about your answer.

● **Practice**

1.   a thing that flies...

- Ⓐ pen
- Ⓑ book
- Ⓒ bird
- Ⓓ cup

4.   to stay on top of water...

- Ⓕ float
- Ⓖ sink
- Ⓗ pin
- Ⓙ zip

2.   a thing that sings...

- Ⓕ chair
- Ⓖ girl
- Ⓗ nest
- Ⓙ paper

5.   noise a dog makes...

- Ⓐ bark
- Ⓑ purr
- Ⓒ cut
- Ⓓ land

3.   to drink a little...

- Ⓐ spill
- Ⓑ tip
- Ⓒ sip
- Ⓓ toss

6.   a food...

- Ⓕ wood
- Ⓖ cart
- Ⓗ apple
- Ⓙ bed

 STOP

Name _____

READING: VOCABULARY

● **Lesson 11: Synonyms**

Directions: Listen to your teacher read the sentence and word choices. Look at the underlined part. Mark the word that means about the same. Practice with examples A and B.

Examples

A.   I was sleepy.

- (A)   tired
- (B)   running
- (C)   tall
- (D)   purple

B.   Jill was in the center.

- (F)   bowl
- (G)   middle
- (H)   end
- (J)   side

Clue   Think about what the sentence means.

● **Practice**

1.   The car was speedy.

- (A)   better
- (B)   heavy
- (C)   fast
- (D)   able

2.   She is lovely.

- (F)   pretty
- (G)   sharp
- (H)   sad
- (J)   near

3.   The soup is steaming.

- (A)   soft
- (B)   spilling
- (C)   hot
- (D)   cold

4.   Kida washes dishes.

- (F)   hides
- (G)   cuts
- (H)   sleeps
- (J)   cleans

5.   It is a small city.

- (A)   house
- (B)   bus
- (C)   town
- (D)   road

6.   We took a boat ride.

- (F)   car
- (G)   balloon
- (H)   ship
- (J)   bike

STOP

READING: VOCABULARY

● **Lesson 12: Antonyms**

Directions: Listen to your teacher read the sentence and word choices. Look at the underlined part. Mark the word that means the opposite. Practice with examples A and B.

Examples

A.   This is wet.
- Ⓐ big
- Ⓑ brown
- Ⓒ dry
- Ⓓ soaked

B.   The rock is heavy.
- Ⓕ cold
- Ⓖ hard
- Ⓗ dirty
- Ⓙ light

 Clue Remember, the correct answer is the opposite of the underlined part.

● **Practice**

1.   **The bear is tame.**
- Ⓐ black
- Ⓑ wild
- Ⓒ hungry
- Ⓓ big

2.   **Susie whispered the secret.**
- Ⓕ yelled
- Ⓖ tapped
- Ⓗ cried
- Ⓙ wrote

3.   **Why is it so little?**
- Ⓐ loud
- Ⓑ bad
- Ⓒ big
- Ⓓ short

4.   **I run very fast.**
- Ⓕ slow
- Ⓖ quick
- Ⓗ around
- Ⓙ loud

5.   **This is easy.**
- Ⓐ less
- Ⓑ home
- Ⓒ simple
- Ⓓ hard

6.   **Jordan was sick.**
- Ⓕ ill
- Ⓖ happy
- Ⓗ well
- Ⓙ tiny

READING: VOCABULARY

● **Lesson 13: Words in Context**

Directions: Listen to your teacher read the sentence and word choices. Choose the word that completes the sentence. Practice with examples A and B.

Examples

A. The _____ was green. It hopped far.

- (A) dog
- (B) rabbit
- (C) frog
- (D) boy

B. The _____ was long. It had 13 cars.

- (F) string
- (G) train
- (H) paper
- (J) hair

Clue When you think you hear the correct answer, put your finger next to it. Listen to all of the choices.

● **Practice**

1. Sam sat on the _____ . He soon fell asleep.

- (A) ice
- (B) chair
- (C) hammer
- (D) nail

3. There are four _____ on the shelf. Tuti read them all.

- (A) cats
- (B) animals
- (C) suns
- (D) books

2. The bee flew to its _____ . It went inside.

- (F) corner
- (G) cup
- (H) hive
- (J) honey

4. The joke was _____ . We all smiled.

- (F) funny
- (G) sad
- (H) blue
- (J) bread

Name _____

READING: VOCABULARY
SAMPLE TEST

● **Directions:** Listen to your teacher read the phrase. Choose the picture that shows what the words mean. Practice with example A.

A. A red fruit

Ⓐ

Ⓑ

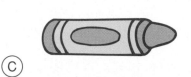
Ⓒ

Do numbers 1–4 the same way.

1. A good pet

Ⓐ

Ⓑ

Ⓒ

2. Summer fun

Ⓕ

Ⓖ

Ⓗ

3. A happy boy

Ⓐ

Ⓑ

Ⓒ

4. Something soft

Ⓕ

Ⓖ

Ⓗ

GO ON

Name _____

READING: VOCABULARY
SAMPLE TEST (cont.)

● **Directions:** Look at the picture. Listen as your teacher reads the word choices. Mark the word that goes with the picture. Practice with examples B and C.

Example

B.

   (F) head

   (G) arm

   (H) hand

C.

   (A) eat

   (B) walk

   (C) wear

Do numbers 5–10 the same way.

5.   (A) frog
      (B) turtle
      (C) kitten

6.   (F) throw
      (G) read
      (H) hold

7.   (A) girl
      (B) bear
      (C) Santa

8.   (F) read
      (G) eat
      (H) paint

9.   (A) bag
      (B) cup
      (C) bowl

10. (F) snack
      (G) ice cream
      (H) mud

GO ON

Name _____

READING: VOCABULARY
SAMPLE TEST (cont.)

●Directions: Listen to your teacher read the sentence and word choices. Look at the underlined part. Mark the word that means about the same.

Directions: Listen to your teacher read the sentence and word choices. Look at the underlined part. Mark the word that is the opposite.

11. **Brenda was chilly.**
- (A) large
- (B) cold
- (C) small
- (D) done

14. **Jetta enjoys music.**
- (F) hates
- (G) likes
- (H) turns
- (J) eats

12. **Bees are insects.**
- (F) bugs
- (G) dish
- (H) hat
- (J) tire

15. **The lion was huge.**
- (A) hungry
- (B) sitting
- (C) small
- (D) fish

13. **Levi made a noise.**
- (A) flower
- (B) shell
- (C) sound
- (D) stone

16. **A turtle is slow.**
- (F) lazy
- (G) fun
- (H) tired
- (J) quick

GO ON

READING: VOCABULARY
SAMPLE TEST (cont.)

●**Directions:** Listen to your teacher read the phrases and word choices. Mark the word that matches the phrase.

Directions: Listen to your teacher read the sentences and word choices. Mark the word that completes the sentence.

17. a thing we eat...

- (A) rope
- (B) orange
- (C) pail
- (D) wheel

18. a wild animal...

- (F) tiger
- (G) butterfly
- (H) fly
- (J) pen

19. a heavy thing...

- (A) feather
- (B) sock
- (C) truck
- (D) balloon

20. The show was great so we

_____ .

- (F) clapped
- (G) swam
- (H) chewed
- (J) blinked

21. I ate the juicy _____ . It dripped.

- (A) bread
- (B) stone
- (C) peach
- (D) book

22. Some _____ fly south in the winter. It is warm.

- (F) bears
- (G) girls
- (H) trucks
- (J) birds

GO ON

Name _____

READING: COMPREHENSION

● **Lesson 14: Listening Comprehension**

Directions: Listen to your teacher read each story. Choose the best answer for each question. Practice with example A.

Example

A. Henry Turtle was in a jam. He had been taking his walk when suddenly an owl landed on his head. What a surprise! What was on Henry's head?

(A)

(B)

(C)

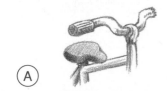
Clue

Listen to each story. Think about what you hear, then mark your choice.

● Practice _____

1. Carol was going to ride her bike. She would go to the park. She asked Ray to go. His bike had a flat tire. What was wrong with Ray's bike?

(A)

(B)

(C)

2. Carol and Ray walked to the park. They walked by the pond. They slid on the slide. They sat on the bench. On what did the children sit to rest?

(F)

(G)

(H)

3. It started to rain. Carol and Ray ran home. They played with Carol's cat. They went to Ray's house. They fed his hamster. What did they play with at Carol's house?

(A)

(B)

(C)

STOP

READING: COMPREHENSION

● **Lesson 15: Picture Comprehension**

Directions: Look at the picture. Listen to your teacher read the words next to the picture. Mark the choice that best describes the picture. Practice with example A.

Example

A.

Ⓐ Butterflies have wings.
Ⓑ I saw five butterflies.
Ⓒ The plane was huge.

 Clue The correct answer says the most about the picture.

● **Practice**

1.

Ⓐ He reads books here.
Ⓑ Three toys are by the chair.
Ⓒ It was dark.

2.

Ⓕ Tiger got a bath.
Ⓖ It was muddy.
Ⓗ I hate to take baths.

3.

Ⓐ Tina has a cat.
Ⓑ Buster chased the kitten.
Ⓒ The cat is hungry.

4.

Ⓕ I gave Mom a hug.
Ⓖ He was sitting.
Ⓗ Gifts are fun to get.

STOP

Name _____

READING: COMPREHENSION

● **Lesson 16: Sentence Comprehension**

Directions: Listen to your teacher read the sentence. Mark the picture that completes or matches the sentence. Practice with examples A and B.

(**Examples**)

A.   This is made of wood. You can write with it.

Ⓐ

Ⓑ

Ⓒ

B.   I ate a _____.

Ⓕ book
Ⓖ cookie
Ⓗ mop

 Clue   Listen to the sentence. Think before you make your choice.

● **Practice**

1.   This is hot. It helps things grow.

Ⓐ

Ⓑ

Ⓒ

2.   You smell with this. It is on your face.

Ⓕ

Ⓖ

Ⓗ

3.   This is my _____ .

Ⓐ dog
Ⓑ school
Ⓒ lake

4.   There is a _____ in front of school.

Ⓕ bike
Ⓖ frog
Ⓗ flag

Name _____

READING: COMPREHENSION

● **Lesson 17: Fiction**

Directions: Listen to your teacher read the story. Choose the best answers for the questions about the story. Practice with example A.

Example

| The boy ran fast. He did not want to be late. Mom was making chicken. It was his favorite food. | **A. What was Mom making?**

 (A) shoes

 (B) chicken

 (C) puddles |

Clue Listen carefully to the whole story.

● **Practice**

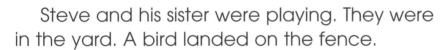

Steve and his sister were playing. They were in the yard. A bird landed on the fence.

They watched the bird fly to the ground. It picked up some grass. Then, it flew to a tree. Steve said the bird was making a nest.

1. Who was with Steve?

(A) Steve's mother

(B) Steve's sister

(C) Steve's dog

2. Where did the bird land?

(F) on the fence

(G) on the roof

(H) under the tree

Name _____

READING: COMPREHENSION

● **Lesson 18: Fiction**

Directions: Listen to your teacher read the story. Mark the best answers to the questions.

Get Warm

Brenda Butterfly was cold. She did not like it. She liked the sunny, warm weather. But it was autumn. "What can I do to get warm?"

Her friend Buddy knew what to do. "I think you should follow the birds. They fly to warm places in winter."

Brenda liked the idea. "That sounds great! Will you come with me, Buddy?"

They followed a flock of birds. It was a long trip. But it was so warm and sunny! Brenda and Buddy smiled. What a good idea!

There were many butterflies in this place. The flowers were colorful. Maybe Brenda and Buddy would stay.

1. **Brenda did not like _____ .**
   - (A) sunny weather
   - (B) being cold
   - (C) her friend Buddy

2. **What did Buddy think Brenda should do?**
   - (F) follow the birds
   - (G) light a fire
   - (H) get new coats

3. **Why should she follow the birds?**
   - (A) to find water
   - (B) to see snow
   - (C) to get to a warm place

4. **Two things Brenda and Buddy liked now were _____ .**
   - (F) their bird friends and fish
   - (G) colorful flowers and being warm
   - (H) flying far and the moon

READING: COMPREHENSION

● **Lesson 19: Nonfiction**

Directions: Listen to your teacher read the story. Choose the best answers to the questions about the story.

Spiders

Spiders are animals. The special name for their animal family is "arachnid." One spider is the tarantula. Another is the wolf spider. All spiders have eight legs. Most spiders spin webs of silk. The webs help the spider catch food. They eat mostly insects. Some spiders are big. There is one as big as a man's hand. Some spiders are very small. One spider is as small as the tip of a pin. This animal is helpful to people. Spiders eat harmful or pesky insects. They eat flies and mosquitoes.

1. **Spiders are _____ .**

   (A) insects

   (B) animals

   (C) plants

2. **Spider webs are made of _____ .**

   (F) silk

   (G) rope

   (H) wire

3. **Why are spiders helpful?**

   (A) Spiders are big and small.

   (B) A tarantula is a kind of spider.

   (C) Spiders eat harmful insects.

4. **Why was this story written?**

   (F) to tell about spiders

   (G) to tell about mosquitoes

   (H) to scare you

READING: COMPREHENSION

● **Lesson 20: Nonfiction**

Directions: Listen to your teacher read the story. Choose the best answers to the questions.

Statue of Liberty

The Statue of Liberty is in New York. It is a famous statue. People in France gave the United States the statue. This happened in 1884. They wanted to show their friendship.

It is one of the biggest statues ever made. The statue is made from copper. It shows a lady. She is dressed in a robe. She is wearing a crown. The lady is holding a torch and a tablet. A poet wrote a famous poem about the statue. It is on a bronze plaque. People read it when they visit.

Long ago, millions of immigrants, people coming to live in the United States, saw the statue. They felt like she welcomed them. It seemed like her torch was lighting the way to their new home. Millions of other people, called tourists, have also visited. They can climb up to the crown. They can see New York City. Many people around the world know about this great statue.

1. **Who gave the Statue of Liberty to the United States?**
   - (A) the people of France
   - (B) many immigrants
   - (C) the queen

2. **Why did they give the statue to the United States?**
   - (F) to make money
   - (G) so the United States would give them one
   - (H) to show friendship

3. **The statue is made from copper because _____ .**
   - (A) copper is ugly
   - (B) it is strong
   - (C) it smells nice

4. **Immigrants felt like the statue _____ .**
   - (F) worked like a flashlight
   - (G) welcomed them
   - (H) was too tall

STOP

READING: COMPREHENSION
SAMPLE TEST

● **Directions:** Listen to your teacher read the sentences. Mark the picture that best matches the sentences. Practice with example A. Do numbers 1–3 the same way.

Example

A. **This is my brother. He has glasses.**

Ⓐ    Ⓑ    Ⓒ

1. **Mother grew pretty flowers.**

Ⓐ    Ⓑ    Ⓒ

2. **It is fun at the park. We love to play.**

Ⓕ    Ⓖ    Ⓗ

3. **Kenny loves bears. They are his favorite animal.**

Ⓐ    Ⓑ    Ⓒ    GO ON ➡

Name _____

READING: COMPREHENSION
SAMPLE TEST (cont.)

● **Directions:** Listen to your teacher read the story and the questions. Choose the best answer for each question.

Kite Trouble

The wind was blowing. Inga wanted to fly a kite. It was sunny and warm. She went to the park. Jesse went with her. They ran all the way to the park.

Inga and Jesse got ready. Inga held the kite. Then, she held the string. A big wind blew the kite high. Inga ran. Jesse wanted to try. When she stopped running, he asked Inga. Inga gave him the string. A big wind came. The string slipped. The kite went very high. The kite was caught in the tree. Inga and Jesse started to cry. They walked home. Maybe Daddy could help.

4. **What did Inga want to do?**

   Ⓕ run with Jesse

   Ⓖ fly a kite

   Ⓗ play in the sun

5. **What kind of weather was it?**

   Ⓐ sunny and warm

   Ⓑ cold and windy

   Ⓒ snowing

6. **How did the kite get caught in the tree?**

   Ⓕ Daddy put it there.

   Ⓖ Inga ran into the tree.

   Ⓗ A big wind blew it there.

7. **Why did Inga and Jesse cry?**

   Ⓐ The kite was in the tree.

   Ⓑ It started to rain.

   Ⓒ Jesse broke the kite string.

GO ON

READING: COMPREHENSION
SAMPLE TEST

● **Directions:** Listen to your teacher read the story and questions. Mark the best answer for the questions.

Apples

Apples grow best where there are four seasons in the year. In the spring, apple trees will have white flowers and small green leaves in their branches. Then, the flowers drop off. Tiny green apples start to grow as the weather gets warm. In the summer, the tree branches fill with small apples that grow and grow. In the fall, the big apples are ready to be picked. Leaves start to drop off the branches. In the winter, the apple tree will rest. It does not grow any leaves or apples. It is getting ready to grow blossoms and apples again in the spring.

8. **What grows on the apple tree branches first?**
    - (F) apples
    - (G) bee hives
    - (H) flowers and leaves

9. **In what season do the apples grow and grow?**
    - (A) fall
    - (B) summer
    - (C) winter

10. **What happens to apple trees in the winter?**
    - (F) They rest.
    - (G) They grow very tall.
    - (H) Farmers cut them down.

11. **Why was this story written?**
    - (A) to tell about winter
    - (B) to tell about farming
    - (C) to tell about apples

Name _____

ANSWER SHEET

STUDENT'S NAME		SCHOOL

LAST   FIRST   MI

TEACHER

FEMALE ◯   MALE ◯

(Name grid bubbles A–Z)

BIRTH DATE

MONTH	DAY	YEAR
JAN ◯	0 0	0
FEB ◯	1 1	1
MAR ◯	2 2	2
APR ◯	3 3	3
MAY ◯	4	4
JUN ◯	5	5 5
JUL ◯	6	6 6
AUG ◯	7	7 7
SEP ◯	8	8 8
OCT ◯	9	9 9
NOV ◯	0	
DEC ◯		

GRADE
① ② ③ ④ ⑤

Part 1: WORD ANALYSIS

A Ⓐ Ⓑ Ⓒ Ⓓ
1 Ⓐ Ⓑ Ⓒ Ⓓ
2 Ⓕ Ⓖ Ⓗ Ⓙ
3 Ⓐ Ⓑ Ⓒ Ⓓ
4 Ⓕ Ⓖ Ⓗ Ⓙ

5 Ⓐ Ⓑ Ⓒ Ⓓ
B Ⓕ Ⓖ Ⓗ
C Ⓐ Ⓑ Ⓒ
6 Ⓕ Ⓖ Ⓗ
7 Ⓐ Ⓑ Ⓒ

8 Ⓕ Ⓖ Ⓗ
9 Ⓐ Ⓑ Ⓒ
D Ⓕ Ⓖ Ⓗ
10 Ⓕ Ⓖ Ⓗ
11 Ⓐ Ⓑ Ⓒ

12 Ⓕ Ⓖ Ⓗ
13 Ⓐ Ⓑ Ⓒ
14 Ⓕ Ⓖ Ⓗ
15 Ⓐ Ⓑ Ⓒ

E Ⓐ Ⓑ Ⓒ
F Ⓕ Ⓖ Ⓗ
16 Ⓕ Ⓖ Ⓗ
17 Ⓐ Ⓑ Ⓒ

18 Ⓕ Ⓖ Ⓗ
19 Ⓐ Ⓑ Ⓒ

Part 2: VOCABULARY

A Ⓐ Ⓑ Ⓒ
1 Ⓐ Ⓑ Ⓒ
2 Ⓕ Ⓖ Ⓗ
3 Ⓐ Ⓑ Ⓒ
4 Ⓕ Ⓖ Ⓗ

B Ⓕ Ⓖ Ⓗ
C Ⓐ Ⓑ Ⓒ
5 Ⓐ Ⓑ Ⓒ
6 Ⓕ Ⓖ Ⓗ
7 Ⓐ Ⓑ Ⓒ

8 Ⓕ Ⓖ Ⓗ
9 Ⓐ Ⓑ Ⓒ
10 Ⓕ Ⓖ Ⓗ
11 Ⓐ Ⓑ Ⓒ
12 Ⓕ Ⓖ Ⓗ

D Ⓐ Ⓑ Ⓒ Ⓓ
13 Ⓐ Ⓑ Ⓒ Ⓓ
14 Ⓕ Ⓖ Ⓗ Ⓙ
15 Ⓐ Ⓑ Ⓒ Ⓓ
16 Ⓕ Ⓖ Ⓗ Ⓙ

17 Ⓐ Ⓑ Ⓒ Ⓓ
18 Ⓕ Ⓖ Ⓗ Ⓙ
19 Ⓐ Ⓑ Ⓒ Ⓓ
20 Ⓕ Ⓖ Ⓗ Ⓙ
21 Ⓐ Ⓑ Ⓒ Ⓓ

22 Ⓕ Ⓖ Ⓗ Ⓙ

Part 3: READING COMPREHENSION

A Ⓐ Ⓑ Ⓒ
1 Ⓐ Ⓑ Ⓒ
2 Ⓕ Ⓖ Ⓗ
B Ⓕ Ⓖ Ⓗ
3 Ⓐ Ⓑ Ⓒ

4 Ⓕ Ⓖ Ⓗ
5 Ⓐ Ⓑ Ⓒ
6 Ⓕ Ⓖ Ⓗ
C Ⓐ Ⓑ Ⓒ
7 Ⓐ Ⓑ Ⓒ

8 Ⓕ Ⓖ Ⓗ
9 Ⓐ Ⓑ Ⓒ
10 Ⓕ Ⓖ Ⓗ
D Ⓕ Ⓖ Ⓗ
11 Ⓐ Ⓑ Ⓒ

12 Ⓕ Ⓖ Ⓗ
13 Ⓐ Ⓑ Ⓒ
14 Ⓕ Ⓖ Ⓗ
15 Ⓐ Ⓑ Ⓒ
16 Ⓕ Ⓖ Ⓗ

17 Ⓐ Ⓑ Ⓒ
18 Ⓕ Ⓖ Ⓗ
19 Ⓐ Ⓑ Ⓒ
20 Ⓕ Ⓖ Ⓗ
21 Ⓐ Ⓑ Ⓒ

22 Ⓕ Ⓖ Ⓗ
23 Ⓐ Ⓑ Ⓒ
24 Ⓕ Ⓖ Ⓗ
25 Ⓐ Ⓑ Ⓒ
26 Ⓕ Ⓖ Ⓗ

Name _____

READING PRACTICE TEST

Part 1: Word Analysis

Directions: Listen to your teacher read each question and the answer choices. Choose the best answer. Practice with example A. Do numbers 1–5 the same way.

Example

A. Which letter does the word **water** begin with?

- (A) t
- (B) v
- (C) m
- (D) w

1. Which letter does the word **heart** begin with?
   - (A) p
   - (B) b
   - (C) d
   - (D) h

2. Which letter does the word **take** begin with?
   - (F) t
   - (G) b
   - (H) a
   - (J) e

3. Which letter does the word **sunny** begin with?
   - (A) c
   - (B) s
   - (C) y
   - (D) l

4. Which letter does the word **bottle** begin with?
   - (F) d
   - (G) h
   - (H) b
   - (J) p

5. Which letter does the word **money** begin with?
   - (A) m
   - (B) n
   - (C) w
   - (D) j

Name _____

READING PRACTICE TEST

● **Part 1: Word Analysis (cont.)**

Directions: Listen closely as your teacher reads each question and the answer choices. Choose the word with the same beginning or ending sound. Practice with examples B and C. Do the same for numbers 6–9.

Examples

B. **Which picture has the same beginning sound as beet?**

(F)

(G)

(H)

C. **Which word has the same ending sound as slip?**

- (A) truck
- (B) sash
- (C) map

6. **Which picture has the same beginning sound as cup?**

(F)

(G)

(H)

7. **Which picture has the same ending sound as Mike?**

(A)

(B)

(C)

8. **Which word has the same beginning sound as table?**

- (F) cash
- (G) shoot
- (H) try

9. **Which word has the same ending sound as frog?**

- (A) gray
- (B) tag
- (C) begin

STOP

Name _____

READING PRACTICE TEST

● **Part 1: Word Analysis (cont.)**

Directions: Listen to your teacher say the words. Notice the underlined part. Listen as your teacher reads the word choices. Listen for the word with the same sound as the underlined part and mark it. Practice with example D. Do the same for numbers 10–15.

Example

D. wig

Ⓕ time

Ⓖ swam

Ⓗ tip

10. pat

Ⓕ from

Ⓖ mad

Ⓗ goes

11. mine

Ⓐ dime

Ⓑ into

Ⓒ hurt

12. pump

Ⓕ child

Ⓖ cutting

Ⓗ shark

13. shout

Ⓐ loud

Ⓑ crow

Ⓒ pill

14. made

Ⓕ bake

Ⓖ puddle

Ⓗ line

15. beg

Ⓐ mass

Ⓑ kelp

Ⓒ broke

STOP

READING PRACTICE TEST

● **Part 1: Word Analysis (cont.)**

Directions: Listen to your teacher read the words. Choose the picture that rhymes with the word. Practice with examples E and F. Do the same for numbers 16–19.

Examples

E.   **Which picture rhymes with barn?**

Ⓐ   Ⓑ   Ⓒ

F.   **Which word rhymes with tool?**

Ⓕ pool
Ⓖ book
Ⓗ lamp

16. **Which picture rhymes with dish?**

Ⓕ      Ⓖ      Ⓗ

17. **Which picture rhymes with car?**

Ⓐ   Ⓑ   Ⓒ

18. **Which word rhymes with chance?**

Ⓕ dance
Ⓖ make
Ⓗ patch

19. **Which word rhymes with how?**

Ⓐ show
Ⓑ now
Ⓒ zoom

Name _____

READING PRACTICE TEST

● **Part 2: Vocabulary**

Directions: Listen to your teacher read the group of words and answer choices. Choose the picture that matches the words. Practice with example A. Do the same for 1–4.

Example

A. Something to eat

(A)

(B)

(C)

1. Something that rings

(A)

(B)

(C)

2. Something to ride in

(F)

(G)

(H)

3. To get taller

(A) shrink

(B) grow

(C) empty

4. A place for clothes

(F) closet

(G) desk

(H) doghouse

Name _____

READING PRACTICE TEST

● **Part 2: Vocabulary (cont.)**

Directions: Look at the picture. Listen as your teacher reads the word choices. Mark the word that goes with the picture. Practice with examples B and C. Do the same for numbers 5–12.

Example

B.
- Ⓕ cap
- Ⓖ box
- Ⓗ jacket

C.
- Ⓐ kick
- Ⓑ throw
- Ⓒ swing

5.
- Ⓐ dance
- Ⓑ run
- Ⓒ sleep

6.
- Ⓕ blanket
- Ⓖ coat
- Ⓗ hat

7.
- Ⓐ one
- Ⓑ two
- Ⓒ three

8.
- Ⓕ dog
- Ⓖ girl
- Ⓗ boy

9.
- Ⓐ sledding
- Ⓑ camping
- Ⓒ shopping

10.
- Ⓕ tent
- Ⓖ car
- Ⓗ van

11.
- Ⓐ hot
- Ⓑ snowing
- Ⓒ raining

12.
- Ⓕ sandcastle
- Ⓖ toothpicks
- Ⓗ jelly

298

Name _____

READING PRACTICE TEST

● **Part 2: Vocabulary (cont.)**

Directions: Listen closely as your teacher reads the sentences and word choices. Choose the word that completes the sentence. Practice with example D. Do the same for numbers 13–16.

Example

D.   Camila _____ the phone.

- (A) ringing
- (B) answered
- (C) went
- (D) shouted

---

13. My mother drinks _____ .

- (A) tea
- (B) nails
- (C) watermelon
- (D) sandwiches

14. The _____ on the radio was loud.

- (F) sun
- (G) water
- (H) music
- (J) computer

15. Lucy walked all the way to the _____ .

- (A) over
- (B) cut
- (C) jar
- (D) park

16. Maisie sat on the _____ .

- (F) touch
- (G) something
- (H) bench
- (J) large

STOP

Name _____

READING PRACTICE TEST

● **Part 2: Vocabulary (cont.)**

Directions: Listen closely as your teacher reads the sentences and word choices. Choose the answer that means the same or about the same as the underlined word for numbers 17–19.

Directions: Listen closely as your teacher reads the sentences and word choices. Choose the answer that means the opposite of the underlined word for numbers 20–22.

17. **Do you like watermelon?**

    (A) make

    (B) enjoy

    (C) hate

    (D) pat

18. **His ideas are always great!**

    (F) wonderful

    (G) crazy

    (H) boring

    (J) bunny

19. **Listen to the story.**

    (A) taste

    (B) hear

    (C) look

    (D) sit

20. **I am wet.**

    (F) soaked

    (G) dry

    (H) yellow

    (J) quiet

21. **Sammy is a tiny mouse.**

    (A) large

    (B) small

    (C) friendly

    (D) brown

22. **The glass is full.**

    (F) mine

    (G) Teri's

    (H) empty

    (J) broken

READING PRACTICE TEST

● **Part 3: Reading Comprehension**

Directions: Listen to your teacher read each story. Choose the best answer for the question. Practice with example A. Do the same for numbers 1 and 2.

> **Example**

A. **Grandfather has a farm. He has many animals. He has pigs, chicks, and horses. He loves pigs the most. Which animal does Grandfather love the most?**

Ⓐ   Ⓑ   Ⓒ

1. **Katie packed her backpack. She took things to eat. She took things to drink. Which item wouldn't she put in her bag?**

Ⓐ   Ⓑ   Ⓒ

2. **Lilo was planting a garden. She had many tools. The tools helped her plant. Which picture shows something that Lilo didn't need when planting?**

Ⓕ   Ⓖ   Ⓗ

STOP

Name _____

READING PRACTICE TEST

● **Part 3: Reading Comprehension (cont.)**

Directions: Listen to your teacher read the sentences. Look at the pictures. Choose the sentence that matches the picture. Practice with example B. Do 3–6 the same way.

Example

B.

F. Todd ate cereal.
G. I love my horse.
H. The weather is nice.

3.

A. The boat sunk.
B. My pen does not work.
C. Tanika swims everyday.

4.

F. Lee gave him a car.
G. My dad has a new watch.
H. I see the clock.

5.

A. We read together.
B. I ran away from my brother.
C. He plays the flute.

6.

F. It was snowing.
G. Parker was singing.
H. I go to the library.

Name _____

READING PRACTICE TEST

● **Part 3: Reading Comprehension (cont.)**

Directions: Listen to your teacher read the sentences. Match a picture to the sentences. Practice with example C. Do the same for numbers 7–10.

Example

C. This floats high. Some people ride them.

(A)
(B)
(C)

7. It was very cold. Mother said to wear these.

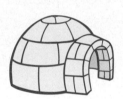
(A)
(B)
(C)

8. It was time. We had to get there fast!

(F)
(G)
(H)

9. One boy is _____ .

(A) whispering

(B) jumping

(C) eating

10. One boy is _____ .

(F) listening

(G) awake

(H) sleeping

READING PRACTICE TEST

● **Part 3: Reading Comprehension (cont.)**

Directions: Listen to your teacher read the story and the questions. Choose the best answer to the questions. Practice with example D. Do the same for numbers 11–14.

Example

Kida's party started at 2 o'clock. It was a pool party. People brought towels. They brought sunscreen.

D. **What kind of party did Kida have?**

   (F) birthday party

   (G) pool party

   (H) sunscreen party

The box was heavy. Simon needed help to move it. He asked Tom. He asked Kate. They went to help. The box was full. It had books in it. Tom and Kate decided to read. Simon sat down to read too. The box stayed.

11. What was in the box?

   (A) Simon

   (B) books

   (C) boxes

13. What did Tom and Kate do?

   (A) read books

   (B) moved the box

   (C) ran away

12. How many people came to help Simon?

   (F) 1

   (G) 2

   (H) 3

14. Why didn't they move the box?

   (F) It was purple.

   (G) They wanted to read.

   (H) Kate went home.

READING PRACTICE TEST

● **Part 3: Reading Comprehension (cont.)**

Directions: Listen to your teacher read the story and the questions. Choose the best answer to the questions.

Riley's Racer

"I want to make a car," Riley said to his father. "Will you help?"

"Yes! We can make a car. We need a plan. We need the tools. Then, we will buy the things we need to make it."

Riley and his father drew a plan for the car. They decided on the size and color. Riley was so happy! It would be big! He could sit in it. It would roll down the hill in the yard. He would wear a helmet.

It took two weeks to make. They had fun. Mom took pictures. She even helped paint the car red. It was a fun family project.

15. What did Riley want to make?

(A) tools

(B) a car

(C) pictures

16. What did they do first?

(F) made a plan

(G) painted

(H) wore a helmet

17. Why would Riley wear a helmet when riding in the car?

(A) to be safe

(B) to hide his hair

(C) to show his friend

18. How did the family feel?

(F) sad

(G) happy

(H) angry

READING PRACTICE TEST

● **Part 3: Reading Comprehension (cont.)**

Directions: Listen to your teacher read the story and the questions. Choose the best answer to the questions.

Ship Shape

A ship is a very large boat. It can travel in the ocean. Some take trips across the whole ocean. Ships carry people and things from one place to another. They have people to work on them. These workers are called the crew.

A ship has many parts. The stern is the back of the ship. The bow is the front. On some ships masts hold the sails. The sails are like big sheets. They catch the wind and help ships go fast. Up on the mast might be a crow's nest. A sailor can sit there. He can watch the ocean.

Another important part is the helm. This is the ship's steering wheel. It can turn the ship to the left and right.

19. **What is a ship?**
    - (A) a train
    - (B) a very large boat
    - (C) a raft

20. **Where do many ships travel?**
    - (F) across the ocean
    - (G) in rivers
    - (H) to dark places

21. **What do sails do?**
    - (A) carry people
    - (B) cover people
    - (C) help the ship go

22. **Why did the author write this story?**
    - (F) to tell about sailors
    - (G) to tell about ships
    - (H) so people would buy boats

READING PRACTICE TEST

● **Part 3: Reading Comprehension (cont.)**

Directions: Listen to your teacher read the story and the questions. Choose the best answer to the questions.

What About Rabbits?

Rabbits are small animals. They have short, fluffy tails. Some have long ears that can hear very well. These ears can be floppy. Some also stick right up!

Rabbits eat all kinds of plants. They eat in fields. They eat in gardens. Some farmers do not like rabbits. They eat the vegetables farmers grow. Sometimes the rabbits eat young trees.

When a mother rabbit is having babies, she digs a hole. She puts in soft grass. She adds her own fur. This will keep the babies warm. She may have two to ten babies. Baby rabbits are called kits.

Some people have pet rabbits. They keep them in pens or cages. They might enter them in contests. Some pet rabbits can be trained to do tricks. Grains, vegetables, and grass are good foods for them.

23. **What is this story mostly about?**
    - Ⓐ rabbits
    - Ⓑ plants rabbits eat
    - Ⓒ farming

24. **Why do some farmers not like rabbits?**
    - Ⓕ They run on the grass.
    - Ⓖ They eat their trees and vegetables.
    - Ⓗ They make too much noise.

25. **Where might pet rabbits sleep?**
    - Ⓐ in a field
    - Ⓑ a pen or cage
    - Ⓒ under the blanket

26. **What are good foods for pet rabbits?**
    - Ⓕ vegetables and grass
    - Ⓖ hot dogs and candy
    - Ⓗ vegetables and meat

STOP

GRADE

1

ANSWER KEY

READING: WORD ANALYSIS

Lesson 1: Letter Recognition
• Page 262
A. C
B. J
1. D
2. F
3. B
4. H

READING: WORD ANALYSIS

Lesson 2: Beginning Sounds
• Page 263
A. B
1. D
2. F
3. C
4. F

READING: WORD ANALYSIS

Lesson 3: Ending Sounds
• Page 264
A. B
B. H
1. C
2. F
3. D
4. H
5. B

READING: WORD ANALYSIS

Lesson 4: Rhyming Words
• Page 265
A. C
1. B
2. H
3. A

READING: WORD ANALYSIS

Lesson 5: Word Recognition
• Page 266
A. A
B. H
1. C
2. G
3. D
4. G

READING: WORD ANALYSIS

Lesson 6: Vowel Sounds and Sight Words
• Page 267
A. A
B. F
1. D
2. F
3. B
4. H

READING: WORD ANALYSIS

Lesson 7: Word Study
• Page 268
A. A
B. G
1. A
2. G
3. A
4. G
5. C
6. G

READING: WORD ANALYSIS

Sample Test
• Pages 269–271
A. B
1. A
2. G
3. C
4. G
5. C
B. H
C. D
6. F

7. B
8. H
9. B
10. G
11. A
12. G
13. A
14. G
15. C
16. F

READING: VOCABULARY

Lesson 8: Picture Vocabulary
• Page 272
A. B
1. B
2. H
3. C
4. F

READING: VOCABULARY

Lesson 9: Word Reading
• Page 273
A. C
B. F
1. A
2. F
3. B
4. H
5. C
6. G

READING: VOCABULARY

Lesson 10: Word Meaning
• Page 274
A. B
B. F
1. C
2. G
3. C
4. F
5. A
6. H

READING: VOCABULARY

Lesson 11: Synonyms
• Page 275
A. A
B. G
1. C
2. F
3. C
4. J
5. C
6. H

READING: VOCABULARY

Lesson 12: Antonyms
• Page 276
A. C
B. J
1. B
2. F
3. C
4. F
5. D
6. H

READING: VOCABULARY

Lesson 13: Words in Context
• Page 277
A. C
B. G
1. B
2. H
3. D
4. F

READING: VOCABULARY

Sample Test
• Pages 278–281
A. B
1. C
2. F
3. A
4. F
B. F
C. C
5. B

ANSWER KEY

6. H
7. A
8. G
9. C
10. F
11. B
12. F
13. C
14. F
15. C
16. J
17. B
18. F
19. C
20. F
21. C
22. J

READING: READING COMPREHENSION
Lesson 14: Listening Comprehension
• Page 282
A. B
1. C
2. H
3. C

READING: READING COMPREHENSION
Lesson 15: Picture Comprehension
• Page 283
A. A
1. B
2. F
3. B
4. H

READING: READING COMPREHENSION
Lesson 16: Sentence Comprehension
• Page 284
A. A
B. G
1. A
2. H
3. B
4. H

READING: READING COMPREHENSION
Lesson 17: Fiction
• Page 285
A. B
1. B
2. F

READING: READING COMPREHENSION
Lesson 18: Fiction
• Page 286
1. B
2. F
3. C
4. G

READING: READING COMPREHENSION
Lesson 19: Nonfiction
• Page 287
1. B
2. F
3. C
4. F

READING: READING COMPREHENSION
Lesson 20: Nonfiction
• Page 288
1. A
2. H
3. B
4. G

READING: READING COMPREHENSION
Sample Test
• Pages 289–291
A. B
1. A
2. H
3. B
4. G
5. A
6. H
7. A
8. H
9. B
10. F
11. C

READING PRACTICE TEST
• Pages 293–307
Part 1: Word Analysis
A. D
1. D
2. F
3. B
4. H
5. A
B. F
C. C
6. G
7. A
8. H
9. B
D. H
10. G
11. A
12. G
13. A
14. F
15. B
E. A
F. F
16. G
17. A
18. F
19. B
Part 2: Vocabulary
A. B
1. C
2. F
3. B
4. F
B. F
C. B
5. C
6. F
7. A
8. G
9. B
10. F
11. A
12. F
D. B
13. A
14. H
15. D

16. H
17. B
18. F
19. B
20. G
21. A
22. H
Part 3: Reading Comprehension
A. C
1. C
2. H
B. F
3. C
4. G
5. A
6. G
C. B
7. C
8. F
9. A
10. F
D. G
11. B
12. G
13. A
14. G
15. B
16. F
17. A
18. G
19. B
20. F
21. C
22. G
23. A
24. G
25. B
26. F

Answer Key

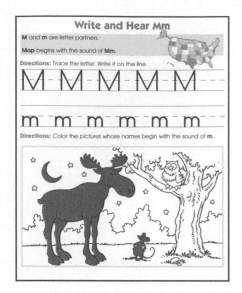

8

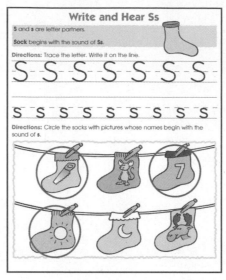

9

10

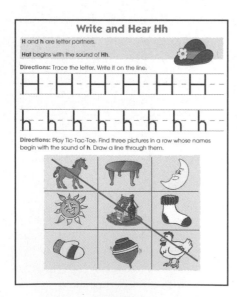

11

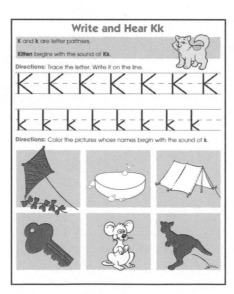

12

13

Write and Hear Ff

F and f are letter partners.

Fox begins with the sound of **Ff**.

Directions: Trace the letter. Write it on the line.

F F F F F F F

f f f f f f f f

Directions: Help the farmer find the fox. Draw a line through the pictures whose names begin with the sound of **f**.

14

Write and Hear Gg

G and g are letter partners.

Goat begins with the sound of **Gg**.

Directions: Trace the letter. Write it on the line.

G G G G G G

g g g g g g g g

Directions: Write **g** If the name of the picture begins with the sound of **g**.

15

Write and Hear Ll

L and l are letter partners.

Leaf begins with the sound of **Ll**.

Directions: Trace the letter. Write it on the line.

L L L L L L L

l l l l l l l l

Directions: Color the leaves with pictures whose names begin with the sound of **l**.

16

Write and Hear Nn

N and n are letter partners.

Nest begins with the sound of **Nn**.

Directions: Trace the letter. Write it on the line.

N N N N N N

n n n n n n n n

Directions: Color the pictures whose names begin with the sound of **n**.

17

Write and Hear Dd

D and d are letter partners.

Desk begins with the sound of **Dd**.

Directions: Trace the letter. Write it on the line.

D D D D D D

d d d d d d d d

Directions: Color the pictures whose names begin with the sound of **d**.

18

Write and Hear Ww

W and w are letter partners.

Window begins with the sound of **Ww**.

Directions: Trace the letter. Write it on the line.

W W W W W

w w w w w w w

Directions: Color the curtains if the name of the picture begins with the sound of **w**.

19

Write and Hear Cc

C and c are letter partners.

Cap begins with the sound of **Cc**.

Directions: Trace the letter. Write it on the line.

C C C C C C

c c c c c c c c c

Directions: Play Tic-Tac-Toe. Find three pictures in a row whose names begin with the sound of **c**. Draw a line through them.

20

Write and Hear Jj

J and j are letter partners.

Jacket begins with the sound of **Jj**.

Directions: Trace the letter. Write it on the line.

J J J J J J J

j j j j j j j j

Directions: Color the jack-in-the-box if the name of its picture begins with the sound of **j**.

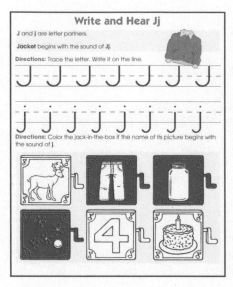

21

Write and Hear Rr

R and r are letter partners.

Ring begins with the sound of **Rr**.

Directions: Trace the letter. Write it on the line.

R R R R R R

r r r r r r r r

Directions: Write **r** on the line if the name of the picture begins with the sound of **r**.

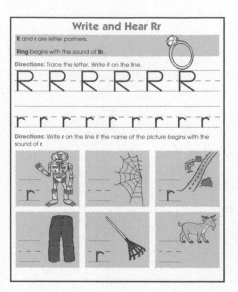

22

Write and Hear Pp

P and p are letter partners.

Pen begins with the sound of **Pp**.

Directions: Trace the letter. Write it on the line.

P P P P P P

p p p p p p p p

Directions: Color the pictures whose names begin with the sound of **p**.

23

Write and Hear Vv

V and v are letter partners.

Vase begins with the sound of **Vv**.

Directions: Trace the letter. Write it on the line.

V V V V V V V

v v v v v v v

Directions: Trace the vases with pictures whose names begin with the sound of **v**. Use a crayon.

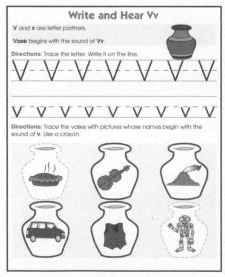

24

Write and Hear Yy

Y and y are letter partners.

Yellow begins with the sound of **Yy**.

Directions: Trace the letter. Write it on the line.

Y Y Y Y Y Y

y y y y y y y

Directions: Play Tic-Tac-Toe. Find three pictures in a row whose names begin with the sound of **y**. Draw a line through them.

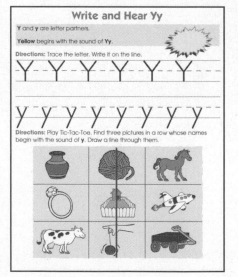

25

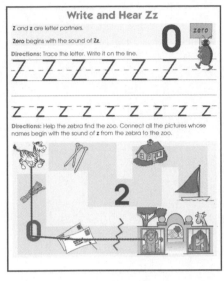

Write and Hear Zz

Z and z are letter partners.

Zero begins with the sound of **Zz**.

Directions: Trace the letter. Write it on the line.

Z Z Z Z Z Z

Z Z Z Z Z Z Z Z Z Z

Directions: Help the zebra find the zoo. Connect all the pictures whose names begin with the sound of **z** from the zebra to the zoo.

26

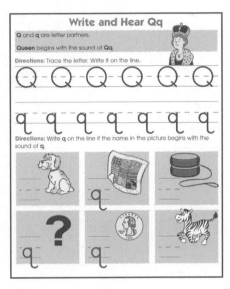

Write and Hear Qq

Q and q are letter partners.

Queen begins with the sound of **Qq**.

Directions: Trace the letter. Write it on the line.

Q Q Q Q Q Q

q q q q q q q q

Directions: Write q on the line if the name in the picture begins with the sound of **q**.

27

Write and Hear Xx

X and x are letter partners.

Box ends with the sound of **Xx**.

Directions: Trace the letter. Write it on the line.

X X X X X X

X X X X X X X X

Directions: Look at the letter at the end of the row. Then, color the pictures whose names end with the sound of that letter. Circle the pictures whose names **end** with **x**.

28

Beginning Consonants: Bb, Cc, Dd, Ff

Beginning consonants are the sounds that come at the beginning of words. Consonants are the letters **b, c, d, f, g, h, j, k, l, m, n, p, q, r, s, t, v, w, x, y,** and **z.**

Directions: Say the name of each letter. Say the sound each letter makes. Circle the letters that make the beginning sound for each picture.

29

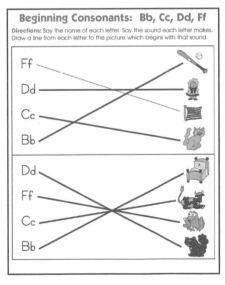

Beginning Consonants: Bb, Cc, Dd, Ff

Directions: Say the name of each letter. Say the sound each letter makes. Draw a line from each letter to the picture which begins with that sound.

30

Beginning Consonants: Gg, Hh, Jj, Kk

Directions: Say the name of each letter. Say the sound each letter makes. Trace the letter pair that makes the beginning sound in each picture.

31

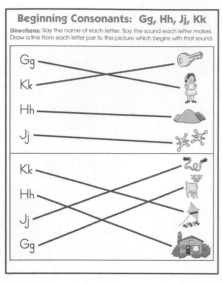

Beginning Consonants: Gg, Hh, Jj, Kk

Directions: Say the name of each letter. Say the sound each letter makes. Draw a line from each letter pair to the picture which begins with that sound.

32

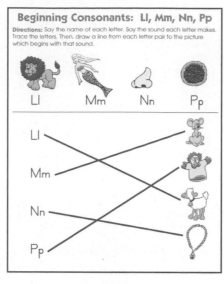

Beginning Consonants: Ll, Mm, Nn, Pp

Directions: Say the name of each letter. Say the sound each letter makes. Trace the letters. Then, draw a line from each letter pair to the picture which begins with that sound.

33

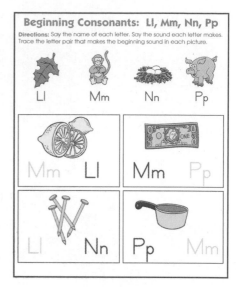

Beginning Consonants: Ll, Mm, Nn, Pp

Directions: Say the name of each letter. Say the sound each letter makes. Trace the letter pair that makes the beginning sound in each picture.

34

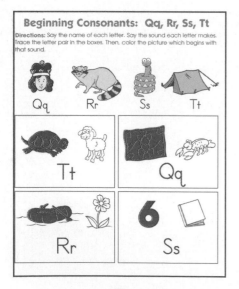

Beginning Consonants: Qq, Rr, Ss, Tt

Directions: Say the name of each letter. Say the sound each letter makes. Trace the letter pair in the boxes. Then, color the picture which begins with that sound.

35

Beginning Consonants: Qq, Rr, Ss, Tt

Directions: Say the name of each letter. Say the sound each letter makes. Draw a line from each letter pair to the picture which begins with that sound.

36

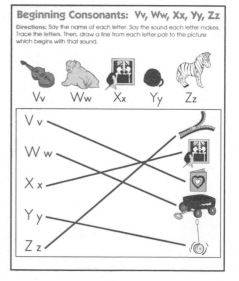

Beginning Consonants: Vv, Ww, Xx, Yy, Zz

Directions: Say the name of each letter. Say the sound each letter makes. Trace the letters. Then, draw a line from each letter pair to the picture which begins with that sound.

37

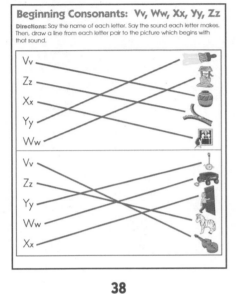

Beginning Consonants: Vv, Ww, Xx, Yy, Zz

Directions: Say the name of each letter. Say the sound each letter makes. Then, draw a line from each letter pair to the picture which begins with that sound.

38

Match Letters and Sounds

Directions: Cut out each letter at the bottom of the page. Find the picture whose name begins with the sound of that letter. Glue the letter in the box beside the picture.

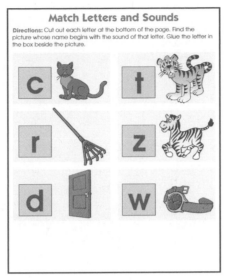

39

How Do I Begin?

Directions: Say the name of each picture. Write the beginning sound for each picture.

_h_ at   _g_ oat   _k_ ite   _j_ am

_j_ acks   _g_ ate   _k_ ey   _h_ appy

Directions: Write each word next to its beginning sound.

g goat   g gate
h hat   h happy
j jam   j jacks
k kite   k key

41

How Do I Begin Again?

Directions: Say each letter sound. Color the pictures in each row that begin with that sound.

b
c
d
f

Directions: Say the name of each picture. Write the beginning sound for each picture.

_b_ ed   _d_ og   _f_ eet   _c_ up

42

Review: Beginning Consonants

Directions: Say each picture name. Circle the letter that stands for the beginning sound.

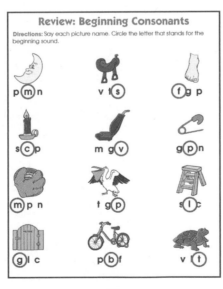

p (m) n   v t (s)   (f) g p
s (c) p   m g (v)   g (p) n
(m) p n   t g (p)   s (l) c
(g) l c   p (b) f   v (t)

43

Review: Beginning Consonants

Directions: Look at the letters in the boxes. Then, say each picture name. Draw a line from the letter to the picture whose name begins with that sound.

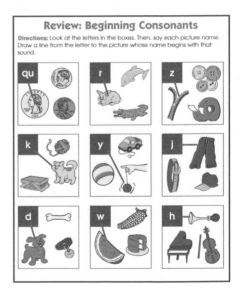

qu   r   z
k   y   j
d   w   h

44

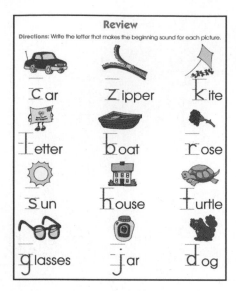

Review

Directions: Write the letter that makes the beginning sound for each picture.

C ar   **Z** ipper   **K** ite

l etter   **b** oat   **r** ose

S un   **h** ouse   **t** urtle

g lasses   **j** ar   **d** og

45

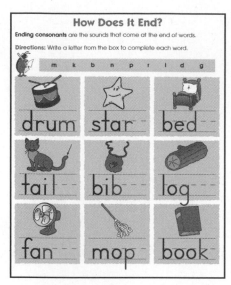

How Does It End?

Ending consonants are the sounds that come at the end of words.

Directions: Write a letter from the box to complete each word.

m k b n p r l d g

drum   star   bed

tail   bib   log

fan   mop   book

46

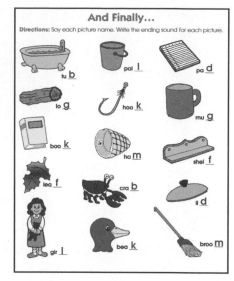

And Finally...

Directions: Say each picture name. Write the ending sound for each picture.

tu **b**   pai **l**   pa **d**

lo **g**   hoo **k**   mu **g**

boo **k**   ha **m**   shel **f**

lea **f**   cra **b**   li **d**

gir **l**   bea **k**   broo **m**

47

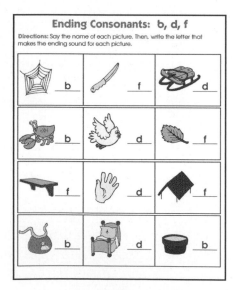

Ending Consonants: b, d, f

Directions: Say the name of each picture. Then, write the letter that makes the ending sound for each picture.

b   **f**   **d**

b   **d**   **f**

f   **d**   **f**

b   **d**   **b**

48

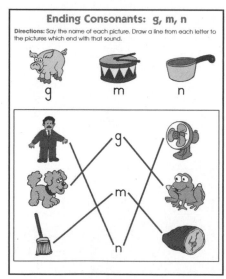

Ending Consonants: g, m, n

Directions: Say the name of each picture. Draw a line from each letter to the pictures which end with that sound.

g   m   n

g

m

n

49

Ending Consonants: k, l, p

Directions: Trace the letters in each row. Say the name of each picture. Then, color the pictures in each row which end with that sound.

k

l

p

50

Ending Consonants: r, s, t, x

Directions: Say the name of each picture. Then, circle the ending sound for each picture.

(star) **r** s t x   (glass) r **s** t x

(car) **r** s t x   (hat) r s **t** x

(gate) r s **t** x   (grass) r **s** t x

(fox) r s t **x**   (skate) r s **t** x

51

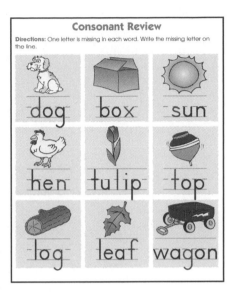

Consonant Review

Directions: One letter is missing in each word. Write the missing letter on the line.

do**g**   bo**x**   su**n**

hen   tu**l**ip   to**p**

lo**g**   lea**f**   wa**g**on

52

Consonant Review

Directions: Write all the missing consonants.

man   fox   pig

bed   jar   camel

goat   car   cap

53

Meet Short a

Listen for the sound of short **a** in **van**.

Directions: Trace the letter. Write it on the line.   van

A A A A A A A A A

a a a a a a a a a

Directions: Color the pictures whose names have the short **a** sound.

54

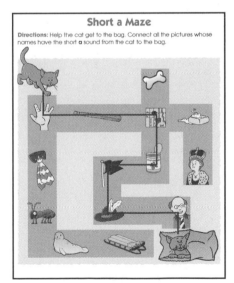

Short a Maze

Directions: Help the cat get to the bag. Connect all the pictures whose names have the short **a** sound from the cat to the bag.

55

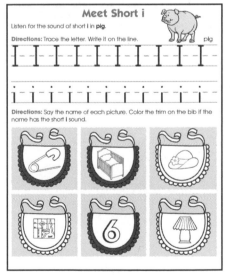

Meet Short i

Listen for the sound of short **i** in **pig**.

Directions: Trace the letter. Write it on the line.   pig

I I I I I I I I I I

i i i i i i i i i i

Directions: Say the name of each picture. Color the trim on the bib if the name has the short **i** sound.

56

Read and Color Short i

Directions: Say the name of each picture. Color the pictures whose names have the short **i** sound. The words in the box will give you hints.

milk	crib	bib
pig	kitten	fish

57

Meet Short u

Listen for the sound of short **u** in **bug**.

Directions: Trace the letter. Write it on the line.

bug

Directions: Say the name of each picture. Color the sun yellow if you hear the short **u** sound in the name.

58

Short u Tic-Tac-Toe

Directions: Color the pictures whose names have the short **u** sound. Then, play Tic-Tac-Toe. Draw a line through three colored pictures in a row.

59

Meet Short o

Listen for the sound of short **o** in **fox**.

Directions: Trace the letter. Write it on the line.

fox

Directions: Say the name of each picture. Write **o** under the picture if the name has the short **o** sound.

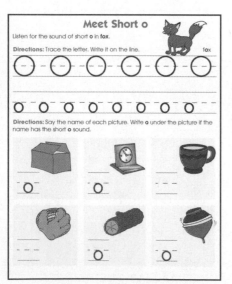

60

Find Short o Words

Directions: Draw a line under each picture whose name has the short **o** sound.

Directions: The words that match the underlined pictures above are hidden in this puzzle. Circle the words. They may go **across** or **down**.

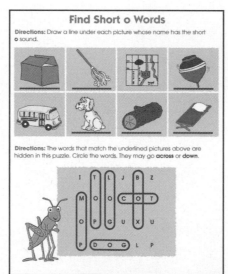

61

Meet Short e

Listen for the sound of short **e** in **hen**.

Directions: Trace the letter. Write it on the line.

hen

Directions: Color the pictures whose names have the short **e** sound.

62

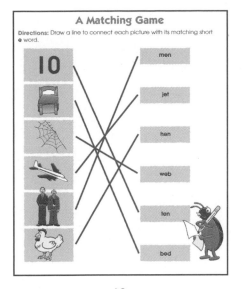

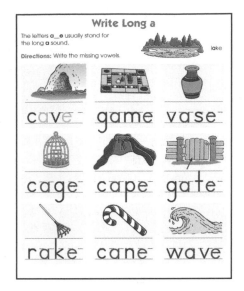

63

64

65

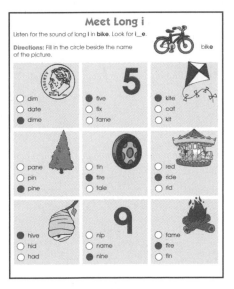

66

67

68

Meet Long o

Listen for the sound of long **o** in **rose**.

Directions: Say the name of each picture. Decide whether the vowel sound you hear is long **o** or short **o**. Fill in the circle beside long **o** or short **o**.

rose

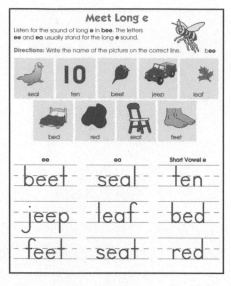

Meet Long e

Listen for the sound of long **e** in **bee**. The letters **ee** and **ea** usually stand for the long **e** sound.

Directions: Write the name of the picture on the correct line.

bee

ee	ea	Short Vowel e
beet	seal	ten
jeep	leaf	bed
feet	seat	red

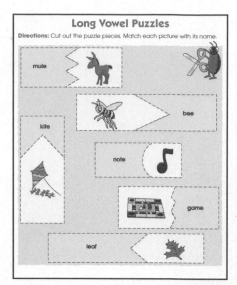

Long Vowel Puzzles

Directions: Cut out the puzzle pieces. Match each picture with its name.

mule · bee · kite · note · game · leaf

69 · **70** · **71**

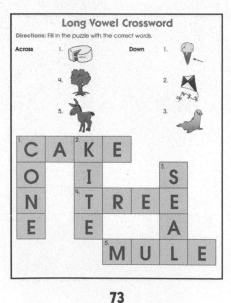

Long Vowel Crossword

Directions: Fill in the puzzle with the correct words.

Across   Down

Long Vowels

Vowels are the letters **a, e, i, o,** and **u.** Long vowel sounds say their own names. Long **a** is the sound you hear in **hay.** Long **e** is the sound you hear in **me.** Long **i** is the sound you hear in **pie.** Long **o** is the sound you hear in **no.** Long **u** is the sound you hear in **cute.**

Directions: Say the long vowel sound at the beginning of each row. Say the name of each picture. Color the pictures in each row that have the same long vowel sound as that letter.

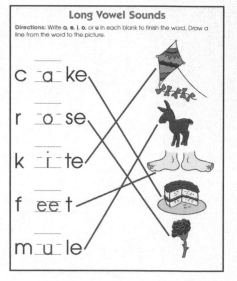

Long Vowel Sounds

Directions: Write **a, e, i, o,** or **u** in each blank to finish the word. Draw a line from the word to the picture.

c a ke
r o se
k i te
f ee t
m u le

73 · **74** · **75**

Super Silent E

When you add an **e** to the end of some words, the vowel changes from a short vowel sound to a long vowel sound. The **e** is silent.

Example: rip + **e** = ripe.

Directions: Say the word under the first picture in each pair. Then, add an **e** to the word under the next picture. Say the new word.

can — **cane**   tub — **tube**

man — **mane**   kit — **kite**

pin — **pine**   cap — **cape**

76

Words With Silent E

When a silent **e** appears at the end of a word, you can't hear it, but it makes the other vowel have a **long** sound. For example, tub has a **short** vowel sound, and **tube** has a **long** vowel sound.

Directions: Look at the pictures below. Decide if the word has a short or long vowel sound. Circle the correct word. Watch for the silent **e**!

can (cane) tub tube   rob (robe) rat rate

(pin) pine (cap) cape   not (note) (pan) pane

slid (slide) dim (dime)   tap (tape) cub (cube)

79

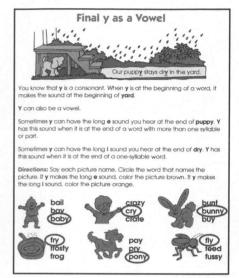

Final y as a Vowel

Our puppy stays dry in the yard.

You know that **y** is a consonant. When **y** is at the beginning of a word, it makes the sound at the beginning of **yard**.

Y can also be a vowel.

Sometimes **y** can have the long **e** sound you hear at the end of **puppy**. **Y** has this sound when it is at the end of a word with more than one syllable or part.

Sometimes **y** can have the long **i** sound you hear at the end of **dry**. **Y** has this sound when it is at the end of a one-syllable word.

Directions: Say each picture name. Circle the word that names the picture. If **y** makes the long **e** sound, color the picture brown. If **y** makes the long **i** sound, color the picture orange.

bail bay (baby)   crazy cry (crate)   bunt (bunny) buy

fry frosty (frog)   pay pry (pony)   fly feed (fussy)

80

Y as a Vowel

Y at the end of a word is a vowel. When **y** is at the end of a one-syllable word, it has the sound of a long **i** (as in **my**). When **y** is at the end of a word with more than one syllable, it has the sound of a long **e** (as in **baby**).

Directions: Look at the words in the box. If the word has the sound of a long **i**, write it under the word **my**. If the word has the sound of a long **e**, write it under the word **baby**. Write the word from the box that answers each riddle.

happy	penny	try	sleepy	dry
bunny	why	sky	party	fly

my	baby
why	happy
try	bunny
sky	penny
dry	sleepy
fly	party

1. It takes five of these to make a nickel.   **penny**
2. This is what you call a baby rabbit.   **bunny**
3. It is often blue and you can see it if you look up.   **sky**
4. You might have one of these on your birthday.   **party**
5. It is the opposite of wet.   **dry**
6. You might use this word to ask a question.   **why**
7. This is what birds and airplanes can do.   **fly**

81

The Sounds of y

A **y** at the end of a word can have the long **i** sound or the long **e** sound. Listen for the long **i** sound in **fly**. Listen for the long **e** sound in **pony**.

fly   pony

Directions: Say the name of each picture. Listen for the sound of **y** at the end of the word. Circle either long **i** or long **e**.

sky — Long i (Long e)   baby — Long i (Long e)   bunny — Long i (Long e)

cry (Long i) Long e   penny — Long i (Long e)   muddy — Long i (Long e)

dry (Long i) Long e   twenty — Long i (Long e)   city — Long i (Long e)

82

Which Sound of Y?

Directions: Say the name of each picture. If the final **y** stands for the long **e** sound, color the picture green. If the **y** stands for the long **i** sound, color the picture yellow.

Finish-the-Word Puzzles

Directions: Write a vowel in the middle of each puzzle that will make a word across and down.

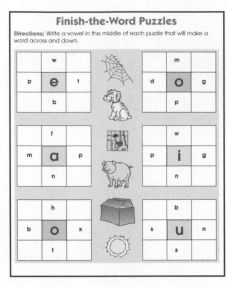

Letter Lift

Directions: Cut out the letters below. Glue each letter on the correct balloon.

83

84

85

Short and Long Vowel Sounds

Directions: Cut out the pictures below. If the vowel has a **long** sound, glue it on the **long** vowel side. If the vowel has a **short** sound, glue it on the **short** vowel side.

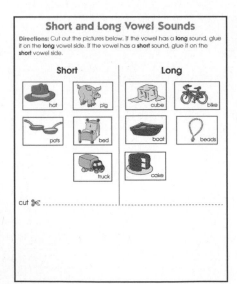

Review

Directions: Color all of the vowels black to discover something hidden in the puzzle.

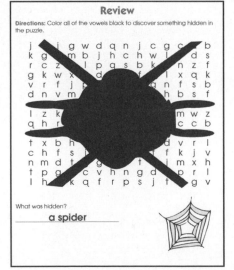

What was hidden?

a spider

87

89

Review

Directions: Circle the word if it has a long vowel sound.

Remember: A long vowel says its name.

(feet) (snake) cup

(hose) (tie) hat

dog (rake) bug

(bone) bib net

90

Review

Directions: Write a vowel on each line to complete each word.

a e i o u

c_a_t b_i_k_e_

sm_o_k_e_ tr_ee_

c_u_b p_i_n

m_o_m b_i_b

d_a_d d_u_ck

91

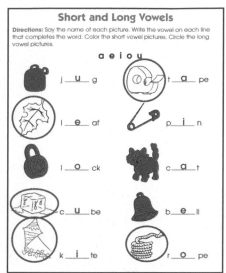

Short and Long Vowels

Directions: Say the name of each picture. Write the vowel on each line that completes the word. Color the short vowel pictures. Circle the long vowel pictures.

a e i o u

j_u_g t_a_pe

l_e_af p_i_n

l_o_ck c_a_t

c_u_be b_e_ll

k_i_te r_o_pe

92

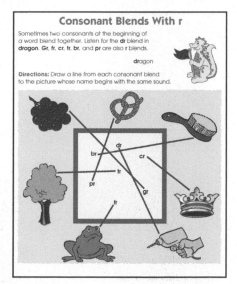

Consonant Blends With r

Sometimes two consonants at the beginning of a word blend together. Listen for the **dr** blend in **dragon**. **Gr, fr, cr, tr, br,** and **pr** are also r blends.

d**r**agon

Directions: Draw a line from each consonant blend to the picture whose name begins with the same sound.

dr
br cr
tr
pr gr
fr

93

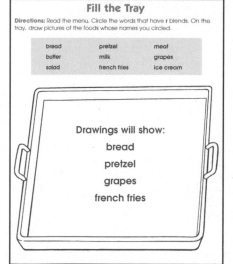

Fill the Tray

Directions: Read the menu. Circle the words that have r blends. On the tray, draw pictures of the foods whose names you circled.

bread	pretzel	meat
butter	milk	grapes
salad	french fries	ice cream

Drawings will show:

bread

pretzel

grapes

french fries

94

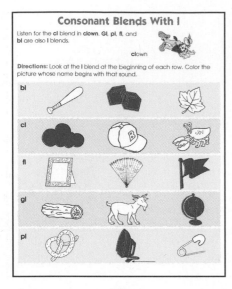

Consonant Blends With l

Listen for the **cl** blend in **clown. Gl, pl, fl,** and **bl** are also l blends.

clown

Directions: Look at the l blend at the beginning of each row. Color the picture whose name begins with that sound.

bl

cl

fl

gl

pl

95

L Blend Tic-Tac-Toe

Directions: Color the pictures whose names begin with l blends. Draw a line through three colored pictures in a row to score a Tic-Tac-Toe.

96

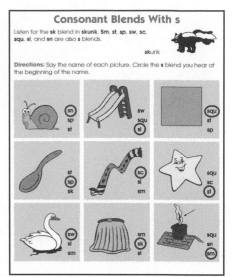

Consonant Blends With s

Listen for the **sk** blend in **skunk. Sm, st, sp, sw, sc, squ, sl,** and **sn** are also s blends.

skunk

Directions: Say the name of each picture. Circle the s blend you hear at the beginning of the name.

97

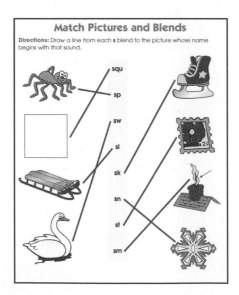

Match Pictures and Blends

Directions: Draw a line from each s blend to the picture whose name begins with that sound.

squ
sp
sw
sl
sk
sn
st
sm

98

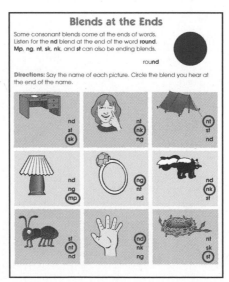

Blends at the Ends

Some consonant blends come at the ends of words. Listen for the **nd** blend at the end of the word **round. Mp, ng, nt, sk, nk,** and **st** can also be ending blends.

round

Directions: Say the name of each picture. Circle the blend you hear at the end of the name.

99

Follow the Final Blends

Directions: Find the notes with pictures whose names end with consonant blends. Color them yellow. Draw a line through the yellow notes from the band to the tent.

100

Ending Consonant Blends

Directions: Write **lt** or **ft** to complete the words.

be **lt**

ra **ft**

sa **lt**

qui **lt**

le **ft**

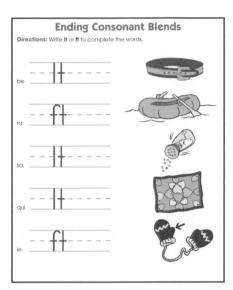

101

Ending Consonant Blends

Directions: Draw a line from the picture to the blend that ends the word.

lf

lk

sk

st

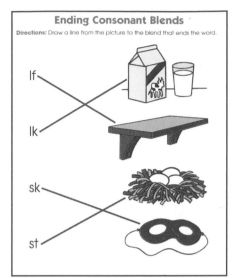

102

Ending Consonant Blends

Directions: Every jukebox has a word ending and a list of letters. Add each of the letters to the word ending to make rhyming words.

____ and
b **and**
h **and**
l **and**
s **and**

____ ent
b **ent**
d **ent**
t **ent**
w **ent**

____ ump
b **ump**
d **ump**
j **ump**
p **ump**

____ ink
p **ink**
s **ink**
l **ink**
th **ink**

____ ing
r **ing**
s **ing**
st **ing**
k **ing**

____ ank
b **ank**
r **ank**
s **ank**
t **ank**

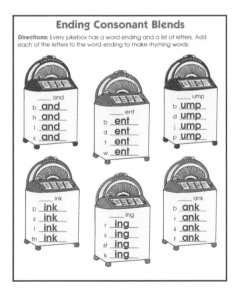

103

Ending Consonant Blends

Directions: Say the blend for each word as you search for it. Circle the letters that make each word.

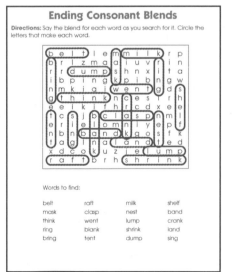

Words to find:

belt	raft	milk	shelf
mask	clasp	nest	band
think	went	lump	crank
ring	blank	shrink	land
bring	tent	dump	sing

104

Review

Directions: Complete each sentence with a word from the word box.

| sting | shelf | drank | plant | stamp |

1. Tom **drank** his milk.

2. A bee can **sting** you.

3. I put a **stamp** on my letter.

4. The **plant** is green.

5. The book is on the **shelf**.

105

Missing Blends

Directions: Fill in the circle beside the missing blend in each word.

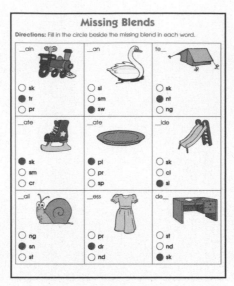

_ain
- ○ sk
- ● tr
- ○ pr

_an
- ○ sl
- ○ sm
- ● sw

te_
- ○ sk
- ● nt
- ○ ng

_ate
- ● sk
- ○ sm
- ○ cr

_ate
- ● pl
- ○ pr
- ○ sp

_ide
- ○ sk
- ○ cl
- ● sl

_ail
- ○ ng
- ● sn
- ○ st

_ess
- ○ pr
- ● dr
- ○ nd

de_
- ○ st
- ○ nd
- ● sk

106

More Missing Blends

Directions: Fill in the circle beside the missing blend in each word.

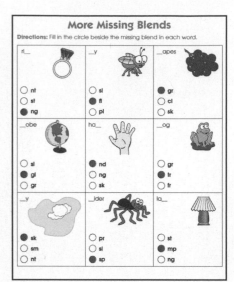

ri_
- ○ nt
- ○ st
- ● ng

_y
- ○ sl
- ● fl
- ○ pl

_apes
- ● gr
- ○ cl
- ○ sk

_obe
- ○ sl
- ● gl
- ○ gr

ha_
- ● nd
- ○ ng
- ○ sk

_og
- ○ gr
- ● tr
- ○ fr

_y
- ● sk
- ○ sm
- ○ nt

_ider
- ○ pr
- ○ sl
- ● sp

la_
- ○ st
- ● mp
- ○ ng

107

Picture Clues

Directions: Read the sentence. Circle the word that makes sense. Use the picture clues to help you. Then, write the word.

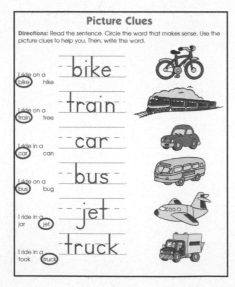

I ride on a (bike) hike — **bike**

I ride on a (train) tree — **train**

I ride in a (car) can — **car**

I ride on a (bus) bug — **bus**

I ride in a jar (jet) — **jet**

I ride in a took (truck) — **truck**

108

Picture Clues

Directions: Cut out the pictures below. Glue them next to the sentences that tell about them.

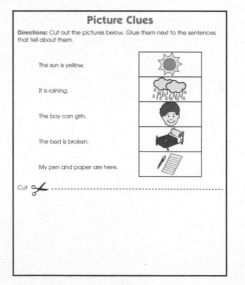

The sun is yellow.

It is raining.

The boy can grin.

The bed is broken.

My pen and paper are here.

Cut ✂ -

109

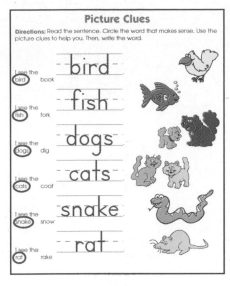

Picture Clues

Directions: Read the sentence. Circle the word that makes sense. Use the picture clues to help you. Then, write the word.

I see the (bird) book. — bird

I see the (fish) fork. — fish

I see the (dogs) dig. — dogs

I see the (cats) coat. — cats

I see the (snake) snow. — snake

I see the (rat) rake. — rat

111

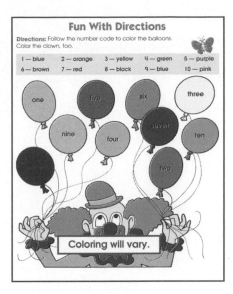

Fun With Directions

Directions: Follow the number code to color the balloons. Color the clown, too.

1 — blue	2 — orange	3 — yellow	4 — green	5 — purple
6 — brown	7 — red	8 — black	9 — blue	10 — pink

one · five · six · three · nine · four · seven · ten · two

Coloring will vary.

112

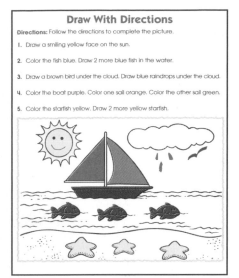

Draw With Directions

Directions: Follow the directions to complete the picture.

1. Draw a smiling yellow face on the sun.

2. Color the fish blue. Draw 2 more blue fish in the water.

3. Draw a brown bird under the cloud. Draw blue raindrops under the cloud.

4. Color the boat purple. Color one sail orange. Color the other sail green.

5. Color the starfish yellow. Draw 2 more yellow starfish.

113

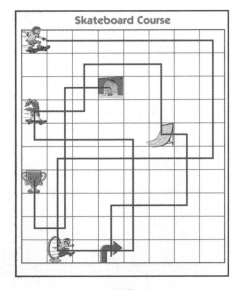

Skateboard Course

115

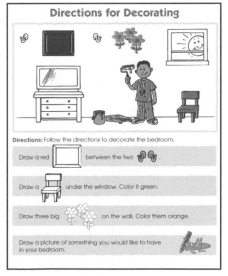

Directions for Decorating

Directions: Follow the directions to decorate the bedroom.

Draw a red [ ] between the two 🩴🩴.

Draw a 🪑 under the window. Color it green.

Draw three big 🌸 on the wall. Color them orange.

Draw a picture of something you would like to have in your bedroom.

117

Following Directions

Read the sentences. Then, follow the directions.

Directions: Bob is making a snowman. He needs your help. Draw a black hat on the snowman. Draw red buttons. Now, draw a green scarf. Draw a happy face on the snowman.

118

Following Directions

Follow the directions to make a paper sack puppet.

Directions: Find a small sack that fits your hand. Cut out teeth from colored paper. Glue them on the sack. Cut out ears. Glue them on the sack. Cut out eyes, a nose, and a tongue. Glue them all on.

Number the pictures 1, 2, 3, and 4 to show the correct order.

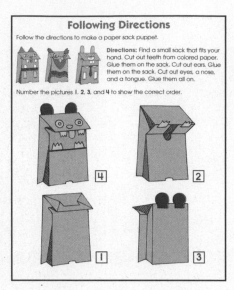

119

Color Code Classifying

Directions: Underline **name** words in **blue**.
Underline **number** words in **red**.
Underline **animal** words in **yellow**.
Underline **color** words in **green**.

pig	Kim	dog	blue
red	green	ten	five
Jack	two	cow	Lee

Directions: Write each word on the correct line.

Name Words
Kim Jack Lee

Number Words
two ten five

Animal Words
dog pig cow

Color Words
green blue red

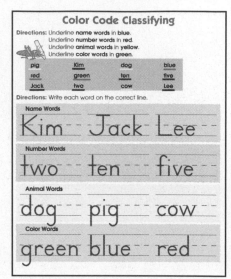

120

Menu Mix-Up

Directions: Circle **names of drinks** in **red**.
Circle **names of vegetables** in **green**.
Circle **names of desserts** in **pink**.

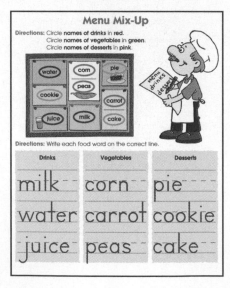

Directions: Write each food word on the correct line.

Drinks	Vegetables	Desserts
milk	corn	pie
water	carrot	cookie
juice	peas	cake

121

Word Sort

Directions: Circle words that name **colors** in **red**.
Circle words that name **shapes** in **yellow**.
Circle words that name **numbers** in **green**.

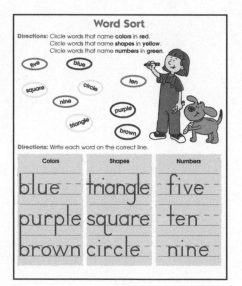

Directions: Write each word on the correct line.

Colors	Shapes	Numbers
blue	triangle	five
purple	square	ten
brown	circle	nine

122

Sort It Out

Directions: Color the pictures. Cut out and glue each picture in the correct room.

Bedroom

Bathroom

Coloring will vary.

Kitchen

123

Where Does It Belong?

Directions: Read the words.
Draw a **circle** around the **sky words**.
Draw a **line** under the **land words**.
Draw a **box** around the **sea words**.

city   rabbit   planet
cloud   forest   whale
shark   moon   shell

Directions: Write each word on the correct line.

Sky Words

cloud moon planet

Land Words

forest city rabbit

Sea Words

whale shark shell

125

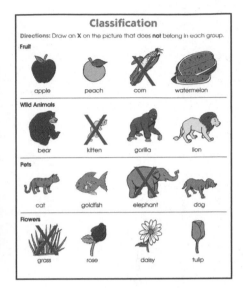

Classification

Directions: Draw an **X** on the picture that does **not** belong in each group.

Fruit

apple   peach   corn   watermelon

Wild Animals

bear   kitten   gorilla   lion

Pets

cat   goldfish   elephant   dog

Flowers

grass   rose   daisy   tulip

126

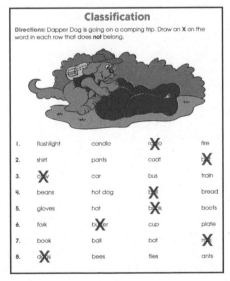

Classification

Directions: Dapper Dog is going on a camping trip. Draw an **X** on the word in each row that does **not** belong.

1.	flashlight	candle	~~radio~~	fire
2.	shirt	pants	coat	~~belt~~
3.	~~cow~~	car	bus	train
4.	beans	hot dog	~~bat~~	bread
5.	gloves	hat	~~book~~	boots
6.	fork	~~butter~~	cup	plate
7.	book	ball	bat	~~mop~~
8.	~~dogs~~	bees	flies	ants

127

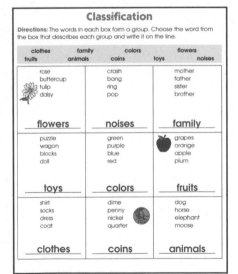

Classification

Directions: The words in each box form a group. Choose the word from the box that describes each group and write it on the line.

clothes	family	colors	flowers
fruits	animals	coins	toys	noises

rose	crash	mother
buttercup	bang	father
tulip	ring	sister
daisy	pop	brother
flowers	**noises**	**family**

puzzle	green	grapes
wagon	purple	orange
blocks	blue	apple
doll	red	plum
toys	**colors**	**fruits**

shirt	dime	dog
socks	penny	horse
dress	nickel	elephant
coat	quarter	moose
clothes	**coins**	**animals**

128

Things That Go Together

Directions: Draw a line to connect the things that go together.

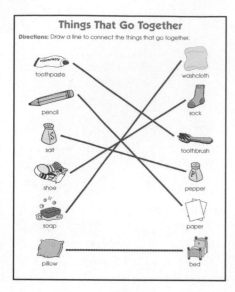

129

More Things That Go Together

Directions: Draw a line to connect the things that go together.

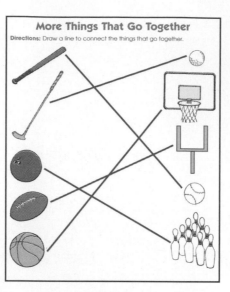

130

Same and Different

Reading to find out how things are alike or different can help you picture and remember what you read. Things that are alike are called **similarities**. Things that are not alike are called **differences**.

Similarity: Beth and Michelle are both girls.
Difference: Beth has short hair, but Michelle has long hair.

Directions: Read the story.

Michelle and Beth are wearing new dresses. Both dresses are striped and have four shiny buttons. Each dress has a belt and a pocket. Beth's dress is blue and white, while Michelle's is yellow and white. The stripes on Beth's dress go up and down. Stripes on Michelle's dress go from side to side. Beth's pocket is bigger with room for a kitten.

Directions: Add the details. Color the dresses. Show how the dresses are alike and how they are different.

131

Comparing Cars

Directions: Read the story.

Sarah built a car for a race. Sarah's car has wheels, a steering wheel, and a place to sit just like the family car. It doesn't have a motor, a key, or a gas pedal. Sarah came in second in last year's race. This year, she hopes to win the race.

Directions: Write **S** beside the things Sarah's car has that are like things the family car has. Write **D** beside the things that are different.

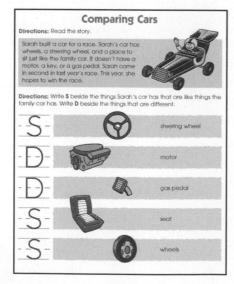

132

Sequencing Pictures

Directions: Put the pictures in each column in order. Write **1**, **2**, or **3** next to each picture.

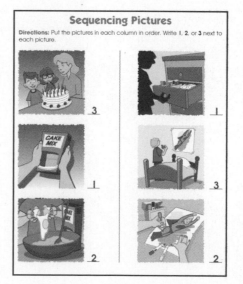

135

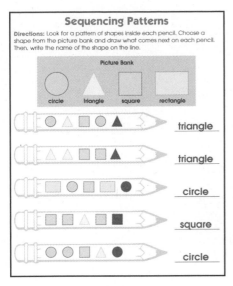

Sequencing Patterns

Directions: Look for a pattern of shapes inside each pencil. Choose a shape from the picture bank and draw what comes next on each pencil. Then, write the name of the shape on the line.

Picture Bank

circle   triangle   square   rectangle

triangle

triangle

circle

square

circle

136

Sequencing Riddles

Directions: To solve the riddles below, look at the letter underneath each line. Next, write the letter that comes **before** each letter.

How do you catch a squirrel?

C L I M B   U P   A   T R E E
D M J N C   V Q   B   U S F F

A N D   A C T   L I K E   A   N U T.
B O E   B D U   M J L F   B   O V U

What has four wheels and flies?

A   G A R B A G E
B   H B S C B H F

T R U C K
U S V D L

Why did the boy run around his bed?

T O   C A T C H   U P   O N
U P   D B U D I   V Q   P O

H I S   S L E E P
I J T   T M F F Q

137

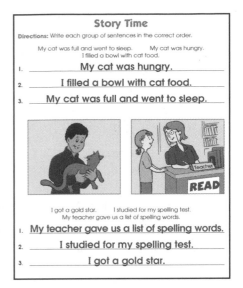

Story Time

Directions: Write each group of sentences in the correct order.

My cat was full and went to sleep.   My cat was hungry.
I filled a bowl with cat food.

1. _____My cat was hungry._____
2. _____I filled a bowl with cat food._____
3. _____My cat was full and went to sleep._____

I got a gold star.   I studied for my spelling test.
My teacher gave us a list of spelling words.

1. _____My teacher gave us a list of spelling words._____
2. _____I studied for my spelling test._____
3. _____I got a gold star._____

138

Sequencing

Directions: Look at the picture story. Read the sentences. Then, write 1, 2, 3, or 4 by each sentence to show the order of the story.

Ben rides the bus. __4__   Ben leaves his house. __1__
Ben is at the bus stop. __2__   Ben gets on the bus. __3__

139

Comprehension: Sequencing

Directions: Kate is sick. What do you think happened? Put numbers beside each sentence to tell the story.

__2__ She went to the doctor's office.
__7__ Kate felt much better.
__1__ Kate felt very hot and tired.
__5__ Kate's mother went to the drug store.
__3__ The doctor looked in Kate's ears.
__6__ Kate took a pill.
__4__ The doctor gave Kate's mother a piece of paper.

140

Sequencing

Tom and Tess are making a snack. They are fixing nacho chips and cheese.

Directions: Look at the picture. Then, look at the steps that Tom and Tess use. Put numbers beside each sentence to tell the correct order.

_5_ Tom and Tess cook the chips in the microwave oven for 2 minutes.

_2_ They get out a plate to cook on.

_1_ Tom and Tess get out the nacho chips and cheese.

_6_ Tom and Tess eat the food.

_3_ They put the chips on a plate.

_4_ They put cheese on the chips.

141

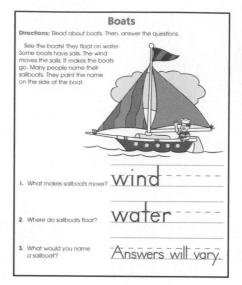

Boats

Directions: Read about boats. Then, answer the questions.

See the boats! They float on water. Some boats have sails. The wind moves the sails. It makes the boats go. Many people name their sailboats. They paint the name on the side of the boat.

1. What makes sailboats move? **wind**

2. Where do sailboats float? **water**

3. What would you name a sailboat? **Answers will vary.**

142

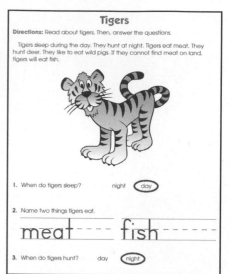

Tigers

Directions: Read about tigers. Then, answer the questions.

Tigers sleep during the day. They hunt at night. Tigers eat meat. They hunt deer. They like to eat wild pigs. If they cannot find meat on land, tigers will eat fish.

1. When do tigers sleep? night (day)

2. Name two things tigers eat.
meat   fish

3. When do tigers hunt? day (night)

143

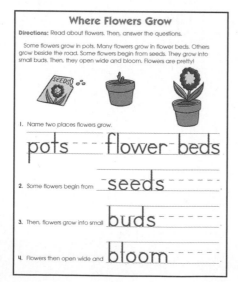

Where Flowers Grow

Directions: Read about flowers. Then, answer the questions.

Some flowers grow in pots. Many flowers grow in flower beds. Others grow beside the road. Some flowers begin from seeds. They grow into small buds. Then, they open wide and bloom. Flowers are pretty!

1. Name two places flowers grow.
pots   flower beds

2. Some flowers begin from **seeds**

3. Then, flowers grow into small **buds**

4. Flowers then open wide and **bloom**

144

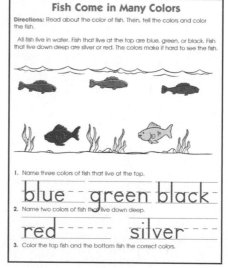

Fish Come in Many Colors

Directions: Read about the color of fish. Then, tell the colors and color the fish.

All fish live in water. Fish that live at the top are blue, green, or black. Fish that live down deep are silver or red. The colors make it hard to see the fish.

1. Name three colors of fish that live at the top.
blue   green   black

2. Name two colors of fish that live down deep.
red   silver

3. Color the top fish and the bottom fish the correct colors.

145

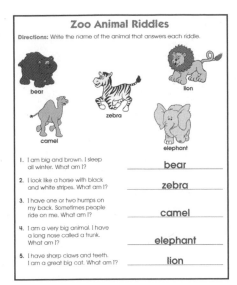

Zoo Animal Riddles

Directions: Write the name of the animal that answers each riddle.

bear

zebra

lion

camel

elephant

1. I am big and brown. I sleep all winter. What am I? **bear**

2. I look like a horse with black and white stripes. What am I? **zebra**

3. I have one or two humps on my back. Sometimes people ride on me. What am I? **camel**

4. I am a very big animal. I have a long nose called a trunk. What am I? **elephant**

5. I have sharp claws and teeth. I am a great big cat. What am I? **lion**

146

Important Signs to Know

Directions: Draw a line from the sign to the sentence that tells about it.

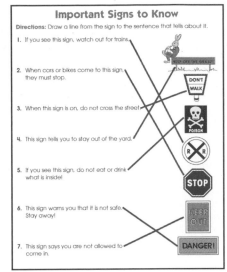

1. If you see this sign, watch out for trains.

2. When cars or bikes come to this sign, they must stop.

3. When this sign is on, do not cross the street.

4. This sign tells you to stay out of the yard.

5. If you see this sign, do not eat or drink what is inside!

6. This sign warns you that it is not safe. Stay away!

7. This sign says you are not allowed to come in.

147

Comprehension

Directions: Read the story. Write the words from the story that complete each sentence.

Jane and Bill like to play in the rain. They take off their shoes and socks. They splash in the puddles. It feels cold! It is fun to splash!

Jane and Bill like to **play in the rain**

They take off their **shoes and socks**

They splash in **the puddles**

Do you like to splash in puddles? (Yes)   No

148

Comprehension

Directions: Read the story. Write the words from the story that complete each sentence.

Ben and Sue have a bug. It is red with black spots. They call it Spot. Spot likes to eat green leaves and grass. The children keep Spot in a box.

Ben and Sue have a **bug**

It is **red** with black spots.

The bug's name is **Spot**

The bug eats **green leaves and grass**

149

What Will Happen Next?

Directions: Look at the pictures.

Directions: Write what you think will happen next.

Answers will vary.

150

What's Next?

Directions: Draw a picture of what you think will happen next in the boxes below.

Pictures will vary but should make sense given the first picture.

151

What Happens Next?

Directions: Read the story. Predict what will happen and circle your answer choice.

David and Fran go the park. The friendly ice-cream man is there selling ice-cream cones. "Hi kids, would you two like an ice-cream cone?" he asks.

Fran and David reach into their pockets, which are empty. "We don't have any money," says Fran. The ice-cream man smiles at them and reaches into his freezer. Then, he says...

1. Ice cream is bad for children.

2. Today it is my treat. Free ice cream for both of you!

3. I am sorry, maybe next time.

Directions: Draw a picture of what you think will happen.

Pictures will vary.

152

What Comes Next?

It's fun to try to guess what will happen next as you read. Guessing what will happen is called **predicting outcomes**.

What you read: Liz drops the glass vase.

What you can predict: The glass vase will break.

Directions: Read the story. Then, follow the directions below.

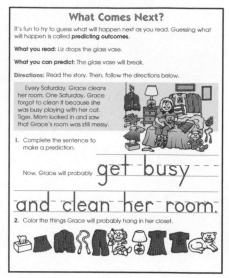

Every Saturday, Grace cleans her room. One Saturday, Grace forgot to clean it because she was busy playing with her cat, Tiger. Mom looked in and saw that Grace's room was still messy.

1. Complete the sentence to make a prediction.

Now, Grace will probably **get busy and clean her room.**

2. Color the things Grace will probably hang in her closet.

153

Inside Out!

Directions: Can you match the outsides with the insides? Draw a line from each picture on the left to its inside picture on the right.

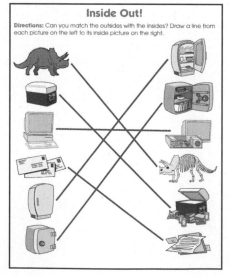

154

Books for Gabby!

Gabby loves to read books about many different topics. She loves to read about exotic animals. She loves stories about famous people. Gabby is also interested in becoming a doctor or an actress one day.

Directions: Look at the books below. Circle only the books that Gabby would like to read.

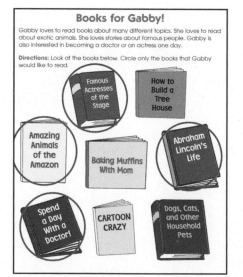

155

Use Your Head!

Directions: Read each sentence below. Then, read each statement that follows it. Using the information in the first sentence, decide which word best completes each statement. Then, write that word on the line.

"Please put on your heavy winter coat before you go sledding," said my mom.

My mom wanted me to keep

warm   cool   (warm)

I put on my coat **before**

I went sledding. (before) after

"Don't forget to bring your glasses, Tom! It will be hard to see the chalkboard if you don't wear them," reminded his dad.

Tom has **poor** eyesight.

good (poor)

Tom is **forgetful**

(forgetful) aware

Tom is going to **school**

(school) basketball   practice

156

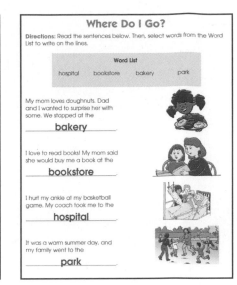

Where Do I Go?

Directions: Read the sentences below. Then, select words from the Word List to write on the lines.

Word List			
hospital	bookstore	bakery	park

My mom loves doughnuts. Dad and I wanted to surprise her with some. We stopped at the

bakery

I love to read books! My mom said she would buy me a book at the

bookstore

I hurt my ankle at my basketball game. My coach took me to the

hospital

It was a warm summer day, and my family went to the

park

157

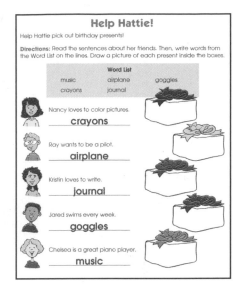

Help Hattie!

Help Hattie pick out birthday presents!

Directions: Read the sentences about her friends. Then, write words from the Word List on the lines. Draw a picture of each present inside the boxes.

Word List		
music	airplane	goggles
crayons	journal	

Nancy loves to color pictures.
crayons

Ray wants to be a pilot.
airplane

Kristin loves to write.
journal

Jared swims every week.
goggles

Chelsea is a great piano player.
music

158

Critical Thinking

Directions: Use your reading skills to answer each riddle. Unscramble the word to check your answer. Write the correct word on the line.

I am a ruler, but I have two feet, not one.

I am a **king**
(ngik)

I am very bright, but that doesn't make me smart.

I am the **sun**
(uns)

You can turn me around, but I won't get dizzy.

I am a **key**
(eky)

I can rattle, but I am not a baby's toy.

I am a **snake**
(nekas)

I will give you milk, but not in a bottle.

I am a **cow**
(ocw)

I smell, but I have no nose.

I am a **flower**
(oerflw)

159

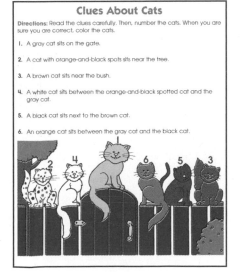

Clues About Cats

Directions: Read the clues carefully. Then, number the cats. When you are sure you are correct, color the cats.

1. A gray cat sits on the gate.

2. A cat with orange-and-black spots sits near the tree.

3. A brown cat sits near the bush.

4. A white cat sits between the orange-and-black spotted cat and the gray cat.

5. A black cat sits next to the brown cat.

6. An orange cat sits between the gray cat and the black cat.

160

Hidden Meanings

Directions: Cut out the cards. Use your thinking skills to match the picture words with their meanings.

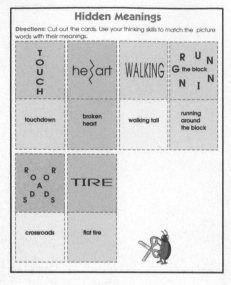

TOUCH	he♥art	WALKING	RU N G the block N I N
touchdown	broken heart	walking tall	running around the block

R O R O A D D S S	TIRE	
crossroads	flat tire	

161

Hey! What's the Big Idea?

Directions: Circle the words that are shown in the picture above.

(bowl)   (spatula)   bed   dog   ink
oven   pan   jar   pot   phone
(mixer)   (napkins)   scooter   (girl)   sneakers
mitt   paper   car   socks   (cupcake)
(spoon)   towels   (cat)   (milk)   tin

Directions: Circle and write the best title for the picture.

Baking With Dad   Chocolate Attack!   Eating Food

Chocolate Attack!

Tell why the other two titles are not as good.

They aren't as clever or as interesting.

163

Picture This!

Directions: Look at the picture. Circle and write the best title on the lines below.

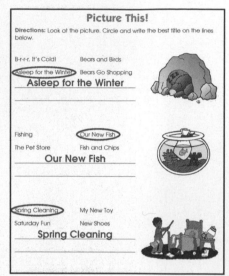

B-r-r-r. It's Cold!   Bears and Birds
(Asleep for the Winter)   Bears Go Shopping
Asleep for the Winter

Fishing   (Our New Fish)
The Pet Store   Fish and Chips
Our New Fish

(Spring Cleaning)   My New Toy
Saturday Fun   New Shoes
Spring Cleaning

164

Picture This!

Directions: Write a title beside each picture below. Your title should tell what each picture is about in just a few words.

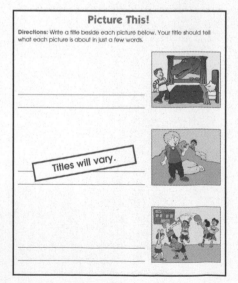

Titles will vary.

165

What's the Main Idea?

The **main idea** tells about the **whole picture.**

Directions: Does the sentence tell the main idea of the picture? Circle **yes** or **no**. Then, write the sentence that best states the main idea for each picture.

The cat wants to play.   yes   (no)
The cat takes a nap.   (yes)   no

Sentences will vary.

The brothers play together.   (yes)   no
The brothers are smart.   yes   (no)

The dog is hungry.   (yes)   no
The dog is playful.   yes   (no)

166

Story Time

The **main idea** tells about the **whole story**.

Read the story below.

"Mom, can we build a fort in the dining room?" John asked.

"Sure, honey," said John's mom. Then, John's mom covered the dining room table with a giant sheet. "Do you want to eat lunch in our fort?" asked John's mom.

"Yes!" said John. Then, John's mom brought two peanut butter sandwiches on paper plates and sat under the table, too!

"Mom, making a fort with you is so much fun!" said John, smiling.

Directions: Does the sentence tell the main idea? Write **yes** or **no**.

1. Then, John's mom covered the dining room table with a giant sheet. __no__

2. "Do you want to eat lunch in our fort?" asked John's mom.
   __no__

3. "Mom, making a fort with you is so much fun!" __no__

4. Write a sentence that tells the main idea: _____
   __John and his mother made a fort.__

167

Caitlin Uses Context Clues

When you read, it is important to know about context clues. **Context clues** can help you figure out the meaning of a word or a missing word just by looking at the **other words** in the sentence.

Directions: Read each sentence below. Circle the context clues, or other words in the sentence that give you hints about the meaning. Choose the answer that fits in each blank. Write it on the line. The first one is done for you.

It was so (hot) outside that I decided I would go to the (beach) and __swim__.

    play   laugh   shovel   swim

"Swim" is the correct answer because of the context clues "hot" and "beach". Now you try.

1. Last night I went to bed very (late) and now I feel __tired__

    happy   hungry   tired   yawn

2. When I (broke) my mom's favorite vase she was __angry__

    worried   nice   magic   angry

3. The clown looked very __silly__ wearing a tiny pink (tutu!)

    silly   smart   orange   light

168

Caitlin Uses More Context Clues

When you read, it is important to know about context clues. **Context clues** can help you figure out the missing word in a sentence, just by looking at the **other words** in the sentence.

Directions: Read each sentence below. Circle the context clues. Choose the answer that fits in each blank. Write it on the line.

1. The (cold wind and lack of heat) made me wish I had an extra __jacket__

    umbrella   toy   shovel   jacket

2. A whale is a very __large__ mammal. Sailors often thought whales were actually (small islands!)

    small   graceful   large   blue

3. Eating fruit is important for __good__ health. Fruit is full of many important (vitamins.)

    bad   good   okay   cat

4. The bus was (very large) and had (a lot) of seats. It could carry __many__ people.

    few   hungry   many   tired

169

Carlo's Context Clues

Context clues can help you figure out the meaning of a word just by looking at the **other words** in the sentence.

Directions: Read each sentence below. Circle the context clues. Choose a word from the word list to replace each word in **bold**. Write it on the line.

Word List		
stop	shined	tease
smart	lively	yummy

1. This prize-winning chocolate cream pie is **delicious.** __yummy__

2. Please do not **taunt** your younger brother. Mean words hurt his feelings. __tease__

3. The police officer told us to **halt** when we came to the red traffic light. __stop__

4. The bouncy, happy puppy was very **energetic.** __lively__

5. The silver bowl really **gleamed** after you polished it. __shined__

6. The **intelligent** girl always got 100's on her spelling tests. __smart__

170

Carlo's Context Clues Continued

Context clues can help you figure out the meaning of a word just by looking at the **other words** in the sentence.

Directions: Read each sentence below. Circle the context clues. Choose a word from the word list to replace each word in **bold**. Write it on the line.

Word List		
petted	understand	tell
little	yelled	

1. "Don't **reveal** the secret! We want the party to be a surprise!" said Mary. __tell__

2. I can't **grasp** that hard math problem! It is too difficult. __understand__

3. The baby bird was so **tiny** that we could hardly see it. __little__

4. We **stroked** the soft kitten and heard it purr. __petted__

5. The crowd **hollered** when the player was called out. __yelled__

171

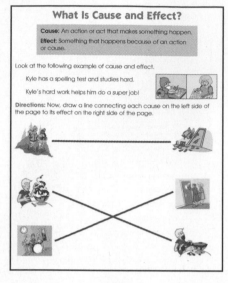

172

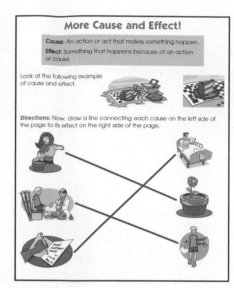

173

174

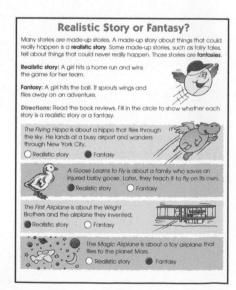

175

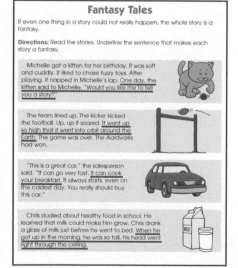

176

Write About Reality

Directions: Write a journal entry. Write about a special day.
You can make u~~~~~~~ Sample answer: ~~~~~~ you
write is somethin~~~

Yesterday our class went on
a field trip. We rode a school
bus to the zoo. We saw lions.
bears. and elephants. My
favorite animals were the
chimpanzees. They made faces
at us. They did funny tricks.
too. We had fun at the zoo.

177

Write a Fantasy

Directions: Write ~~~~~~~~~~~~ Write about
the same specia~~ Sample answer: ~~~~~~~
This time, add de~~~~~~~~

Yesterday our class went on a field trip.
We rode a school bus to the zoo. In the
afternoon. it got very hot. I took off my
hat and my jacket. Then. I watched the
chimpanzees. One chimp seemed to be
looking at me. It did everything I did. I
must have left my hat and jacket by the
chimp's cage. The next thing I knew. the
chimp was wearing my clothes. Nobody
noticed when he climbed onto the school
bus behind me. Now he is a regular
member of the class. He is the class
clown.

178

Penguins

A penguin is a bird that cannot fly. Its wings look and act like flippers. Penguins are very good swimmers and spend a lot of time in the water. White belly feathers and short black feathers on their backs make it hard to spot them in the water. They waddle when they walk. Most wild penguins live in the southern part of the world.

Female penguins lay one to three eggs. The male carries the eggs on his feet and covers them with rolls of body fat to keep them warm. A baby penguin is called a *chick* when it is hatched. Most penguins can live for almost twenty years.

Directions: After reading about penguins, decide if each statement is a fact or an opinion. Write **F** for fact and **O** for opinion.

O 1. A penguin is a beautiful bird.

F 2. A penguin is a bird that cannot fly.

F 3. Penguins are good swimmers.

F 4. Baby penguins are called chicks.

O 5. Female penguins are good nest builders.

O 6. It is fun to watch penguins swimming.

O 7. Bird watchers like to watch penguins.

F 8. A penguin may live for twenty years.

179

Starfish

A starfish is not really a fish. It is an animal. It belongs to a group of animals that have skin that is tough and covered with sharp bumps called *spines*.

Starfish live in the ocean.

Most starfish have five "arms" going out from the main body. This makes them look like stars. The mouth of a starfish is on the underside of its body. A starfish can eat in two different ways. It can take food in through its mouth and eat it. It can also eat by pushing its stomach out of its mouth and wrapping it around the food.

If an arm breaks off the starfish, it can grow a new one.

Directions: Read the statements. Decide if each is a fact or an opinion. Write **F** for fact and **O** for opinion.

O 1. It would be fun to feel a starfish.

O 2. A starfish would be a good pet.

F 3. If a starfish "arm" breaks off, it can grow a new one.

O 4. Starfish look pretty.

F 5. Starfish live in the ocean.

F 6. Starfish have tough skin with spines.

180

Figs

Fig is the name of a fruit and of the plant the fruit grows on. The plant can look like a bush or like a tree. Fig plants grow where it is warm all year long.

The fig fruit grows in bunches on the stems of fig plants. Some figs can be picked two times each year.

They can be picked from old branches in June or July. They can be picked from new branches in August or September.

Many people like to eat figs. They can be eaten in fig cookies or in fig bars. They can be canned or eaten fresh. Sometimes figs are dried.

Directions: Color the fig **red** if the sentence is a **fact**. Color the fig **blue** if the sentence is an **opinion**.

1. A fig is a plant and a fruit.

2. The fig tree is very pretty.

3. Fig plants do not grow where it is very cold.

4. Figs grow in a bunch.

5. You can pick figs two times each year.

6. Figs taste very good.

7. You can eat figs in many ways.

8. The best way to eat a fig is in a fig cookie.

181

What's My Name?

Different words have different jobs. A **naming word** names a person, place, or thing. Naming words are also called **nouns**.

Example: person — nurse
place — store
thing — drum

Directions: In the word box below, circle only the words that name a person, place, or thing. Then, use the nouns you circled to name each picture.

(teacher) up (dog) the (library)
runs is (cowhand) (cap) (zoo)

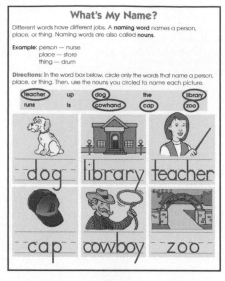

dog   library   teacher

cap   cowboy   zoo

182

Person, Place, or Thing?

Directions: Write each noun in the correct box below.

girl	park	truck	vase
artist	tree	doctor	zoo
school	store	ball	baby

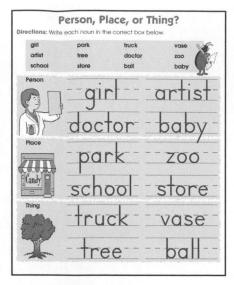

Person

girl   artist
doctor   baby

Place

park   zoo
school   store

Thing

truck   vase
tree   ball

183

Finding Nouns

A **noun** names a person, place, or thing.

Directions: Circle two nouns in each sentence below. The first one is done for you.

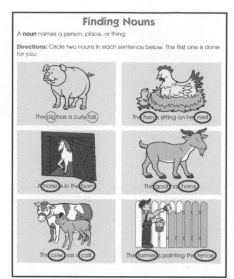

The (pig) has a curly (tail).   The (hen) is sitting on her (nest).

A (horse) is in the (barn).   The (goat) has (horns).

The (cow) has a (calf).   The (farmer) is painting the (fence).

184

Nouns at Play

Directions: Complete each sentence with the correct noun from the word box. Write the noun on the line.

| ducks | sun | tree |
| dog | boys | bird |

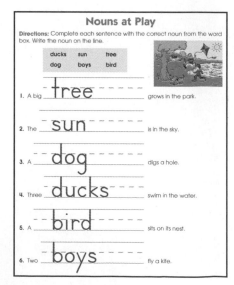

1. A big __tree__ grows in the park.

2. The __sun__ is in the sky.

3. A __dog__ digs a hole.

4. Three __ducks__ swim in the water.

5. A __bird__ sits on its nest.

6. Two __boys__ fly a kite.

185

Nouns

Directions: Complete each sentence with a noun.

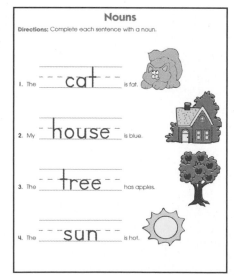

1. The __cat__ is fat.

2. My __house__ is blue.

3. The __tree__ has apples.

4. The __sun__ is hot.

186

Nouns

Directions: Write these naming words in the correct box.

| store | zoo | child | baby | teacher | table |
| cat | park | gym | woman | sock | horse |

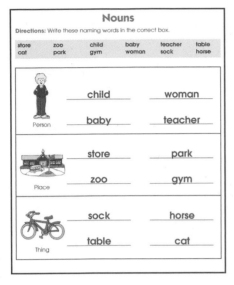

Person

| child | woman |
| baby | teacher |

Place

| store | park |
| zoo | gym |

Thing

| sock | horse |
| table | cat |

187

Verbs

Directions: Look at the picture and read the words. Write an action word in each sentence below.

1. The two boys like to _____ **talk** _____ together.

2. The children _____ **kick** _____ the soccer ball.

3. Some children like to _____ **swing** _____ on the swing.

4. The girl can _____ **run** _____ very fast.

5. The teacher _____ **rings** _____ the bell.

188

Ready, Set, Go!

An **action word** tells what a person or thing can do.

Example: Fred **kicks** the ball.

Directions: Read the words below. Circle words that tell what the children are doing.

jump boy
sleep bed
hello talk
skate mittens
hop sidewalk
sing song
swim deep
story read

189

Action Words

Directions: Underline the action word in each sentence. Then, draw a line to match each sentence with the correct picture. The first one is done for you.

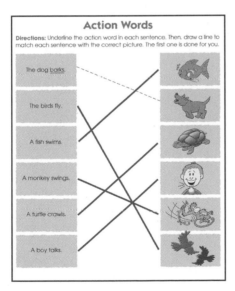

The dog barks.

The birds fly.

A fish swims.

A monkey swings.

A turtle crawls.

A boy talks.

190

What Is a Verb?

A **verb** is an action word. A verb tells what a person or thing does.

Example: Jane **reads** a book.

Directions: Circle the verb in each sentence below.

Two tiny dogs dance.

The bear climbs a ladder.

The clown falls down.

A tiger jumps through a ring.

A boy eats popcorn.

A woman swings on a trapeze.

191

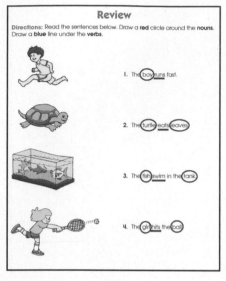

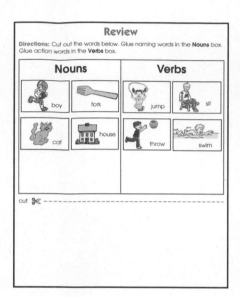

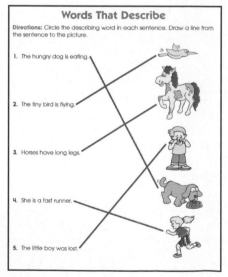

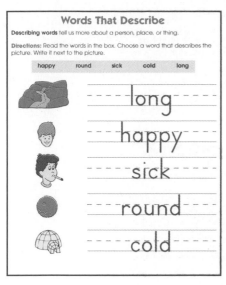

Words That Describe

Describing words tell us more about a person, place, or thing.

Directions: Read the words in the box. Choose a word that describes the picture. Write it next to the picture.

happy	round	sick	cold	long

long
happy
sick
round
cold

198

Adjectives

Describing words are also called **adjectives**.

Directions: Circle the describing words in the sentences.

1. The (juicy) apple is on the plate.
2. The (furry) dog is eating a bone.
3. It was a (sunny) day.
4. The kitten drinks (warm) milk.
5. The baby has a (loud) cry.

199

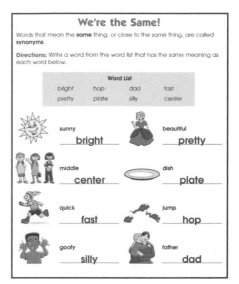

We're the Same!

Words that mean the **same** thing, or close to the same thing, are called **synonyms**.

Directions: Write a word from the word list that has the same meaning as each word below.

Word List

bright	hop	dad	fast
pretty	plate	silly	center

sunny — **bright** | beautiful — **pretty**
middle — **center** | dish — **plate**
quick — **fast** | jump — **hop**
goofy — **silly** | father — **dad**

200

Synonym Squares!

Directions: Circle the **synonym** in each square that has the same meaning or close to the same meaning as the word in **bold** print. The first one is done for you.

end **start**	scream **shout**	cat **sick**
(begin)	brother	both
stop	talk	(ill)

Directions: Think of a synonym for each of the three listed words. Then, write a sentence using **both** words in your sentence.

smart/ _____

Synonyms and sentences will vary.

bad/ _____

little/ _____

201

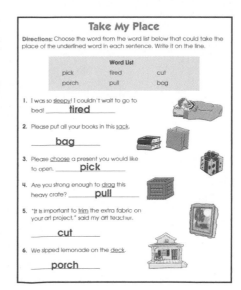

Take My Place

Directions: Choose the word from the word list below that could take the place of the underlined word in each sentence. Write it on the line.

Word List

pick	tired	cut
porch	pull	bag

1. I was so sleepy! I couldn't wait to go to bed! **tired**
2. Please put all your books in this sack. **bag**
3. Please choose a present you would like to open. **pick**
4. Are you strong enough to drag this heavy crate? **pull**
5. "It is important to trim the extra fabric on your art project," said my art teacher. **cut**
6. We sipped lemonade on the deck. **porch**

202

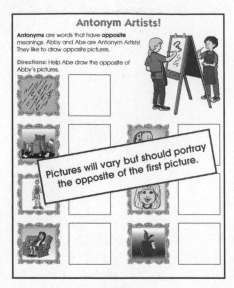

Antonym Artists!

Antonyms are words that have **opposite** meanings. Abby and Abe are Antonym Artists! They like to draw opposite pictures.

Directions: Help Abe draw the opposite of Abby's pictures.

Pictures will vary but should portray the opposite of the first picture.

203

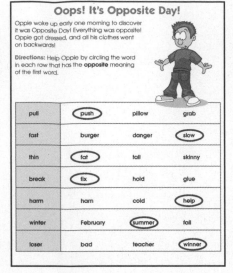

Oops! It's Opposite Day!

Oppie woke up early one morning to discover it was Opposite Day! Everything was opposite! Oppie got dressed, and all his clothes went on backwards!

Directions: Help Oppie by circling the word in each row that has the **opposite** meaning of the first word.

pull	(push)	pillow	grab
fast	burger	danger	(slow)
thin	(fat)	tall	skinny
break	(fix)	hold	glue
harm	harn	cold	(help)
winter	February	(summer)	fall
loser	bad	teacher	(winner)

204

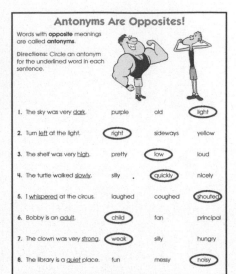

Antonyms Are Opposites!

Words with **opposite** meanings are called **antonyms**.

Directions: Circle an antonym for the underlined word in each sentence.

1. The sky was very <u>dark</u>.   purple   old   (light)
2. Turn <u>left</u> at the light.   (right)   sideways   yellow
3. The shelf was very <u>high</u>.   pretty   (low)   loud
4. The turtle walked <u>slowly</u>.   silly   (quickly)   nicely
5. I <u>whispered</u> at the circus.   laughed   coughed   (shouted)
6. Bobby is an <u>adult</u>.   (child)   fan   principal
7. The clown was very <u>strong</u>.   (weak)   silly   hungry
8. The library is a <u>quiet</u> place.   fun   messy   (noisy)

205

Batty Bats!

Some words have more than one meaning.

The word **bat** has more than one meaning.

Directions: Look at the words and their meanings below. Next to each picture, write the number that has the correct meaning.

can: 1. a metal container   2. to know how

 1   2

band: 1. a group of musicians   2. a strip of material

 1   2

cap: 1. a soft hat with a visor   2. lid or cover

 2   1

crow: 1. a large black bird   2. the loud cry of a rooster

 2   1

206

Match That Meaning!

Some words have more than one meaning. Look at the list of words.

Directions: Match the word's correct meaning to the pictures below.

cross: 1. to draw a line through   2. angry

fall: 3. the season between summer and winter   4. to trip or stumble

land: 5. to bring to a stop or rest   6. the ground

 4   5   1

 6   2   3

207

Match That Meaning!

The word **may** has more than one meaning.

May or 1. the fifth month of the year
may: 2. to be permitted or allowed to do something

May I please have a drink of water?

MAY *(calendar)*

Directions: Write the letter of the correct meaning in each blank.

1. My dad's birthday is in ___1___ .

2. ___2___ I please go to the gym?

3. Many flowers bloom in ___1___ .

4. Mother, ___2___ I go to the swimming party?

5. My brother will come home from college in ___1___ .

208

Homonyms

Homonyms are words that sound the same, but are spelled differently and have different meanings. For example, **sun** and **son** are homonyms.

Directions: Look at the word. Circle the picture that goes with the word.

1. sun
2. hi
3. ate
4. four
5. buy
6. hear

209

Homonyms

Directions: Look at each picture. Circle the homonym that is spelled the correct way.

(deer) dear   blue (blew)

to (two)   hi (high)

by (bye)   new knew

ate (eight)   red (read)

210

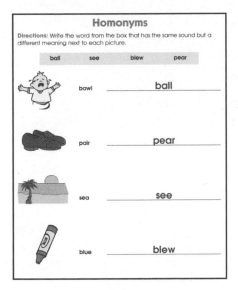

Homonyms

Directions: Write the word from the box that has the same sound but a different meaning next to each picture.

ball	see	blew	pear

bowl ___ball___

pair ___pear___

sea ___see___

blue ___blew___

211

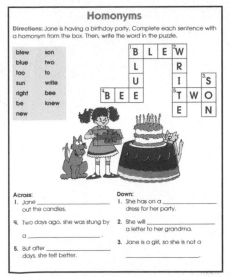

Homonyms

Directions: Jane is having a birthday party. Complete each sentence with a homonym from the box. Then, write the word in the puzzle.

blew	son
blue	two
too	to
sun	write
right	bee
be	knew
new	

Crossword: B L E W / W R I T E / B E E / T W O / S O N (B L U E down)

Across:
1. Jane _____ out the candles.
4. Two days ago, she was stung by a _____ .
5. But after _____ days, she felt better.

Down:
1. She has on a _____ dress for her party.
2. She will _____ a letter to her grandma.
3. Jane is a girl, so she is not a _____ .

212

Make Compound Words

Some short words can be put together to make one new word. The new word is called a **compound word**.

cow + hand = cowhand

Directions: Look at each pair of pictures and words below. Join the two words to make a compound word. Write it on the line.

rain + coat = raincoat

door + bell = doorbell

dog + house = doghouse

pan + cake = pancake

horse + shoe = horseshoe

213

Two Words in One

Directions: Write the two words that make up each compound word below.

snowball	snow	ball
raincoat	rain	coat
airplane	air	plane
watermelon	water	melon
haircut	hair	cut
football	foot	ball
sunshine	sun	shine

214

Compound Word Riddles

Directions: Underline the two words in each sentence that can make a compound word. Write the compound word on the line to complete the sentence.

A kind of bird that is black is a
blackbird

A horse that can race is a
racehorse

A cloth that covers a table is a
tablecloth

A room with a bed is a
bedroom

A book with a story is a
storybook

A bowl that holds fish is a
fishbowl

215

Compound Words

Directions: Look at the pictures and the two words that are next to each other. Put the words together to make a new word. Write the new word.

Example:

house + boat = houseboat

side walk = sidewalk

lip stick = lipstick

sand box = sandbox

lunch box = lunchbox

216

Compound Words

Directions: Cut out the pictures and words at the bottom of the page. Put two words together to make a compound word. Write the new word.

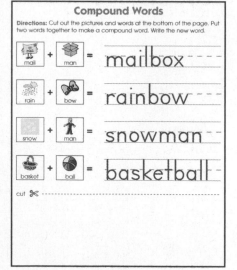

mail + man = mailbox

rain + bow = rainbow

snow + man = snowman

basket + ball = basketball

cut ✂ -

217

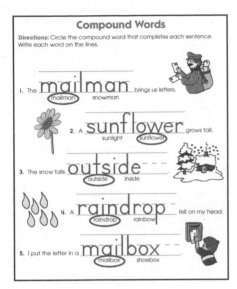

Compound Words

Directions: Circle the compound word that completes each sentence. Write each word on the lines.

1. The **mailman** brings us letters.
   (mailman) snowman

2. A **sunflower** grows tall.
   sunlight (sunflower)

3. The snow falls **outside**
   (outside) inside

4. A **raindrop** fell on my head.
   (raindrop) rainbow

5. I put the letter in a **mailbox**
   (mailbox) shoebox

219

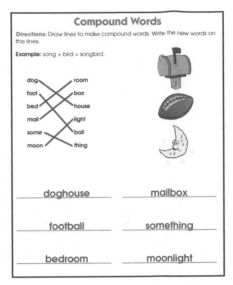

Compound Words

Directions: Draw lines to make compound words. Write the new words on the lines.

Example: song + bird = songbird.

dog — room
foot — box
bed — house
mail — light
some — ball
moon — thing

doghouse   **mailbox**

football   **something**

bedroom   **moonlight**

220

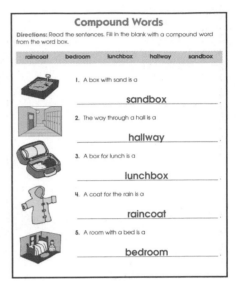

Compound Words

Directions: Read the sentences. Fill in the blank with a compound word from the word box.

| raincoat | bedroom | lunchbox | hallway | sandbox |

1. A box with sand is a
   sandbox

2. The way through a hall is a
   hallway

3. A box for lunch is a
   lunchbox

4. A coat for the rain is a
   raincoat

5. A room with a bed is a
   bedroom

221

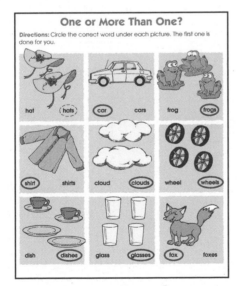

One or More Than One?

Directions: Circle the correct word under each picture. The first one is done for you.

hat (hats)   (car) cars   frog (frogs)

(shirt) shirts   cloud (clouds)   wheel (wheels)

dish (dishes)   glass (glasses)   (fox) foxes

222

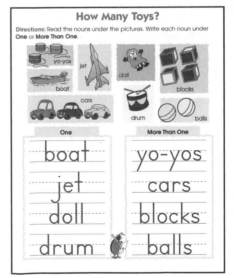

How Many Toys?

Directions: Read the nouns under the pictures. Write each noun under **One** or **More Than One**.

yo-yos   jet   doll   blocks
boat   cars   drum   balls

One	More Than One
boat	yo-yos
jet	cars
doll	blocks
drum	balls

223

Making Nouns Plural

A **plural noun** means more than one. Add **s** to most nouns to make plural nouns.

Example: Penny has one **dog**.
Jerry has two **dogs**.

Directions: Write the plural form of the nouns below.

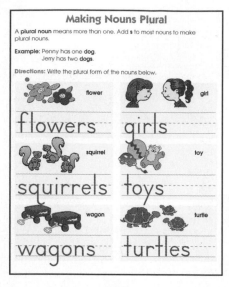

flower — flowers

girl — girls

squirrel — squirrels

toy — toys

wagon — wagons

turtle — turtles

224

More Than One

Some nouns name more than one person, place, or thing.

Directions: Add **s** to make the words tell about the picture.

frog **s**

pan **s**

boy **s**

egg **s**

horn **s**

girl **s**

225

More Than One

An **s** at the end of a word often means there is more than one. Words that mean more than one are also called **plurals**.

Directions: Look at each picture and circle the correct word. Write the word on the line.

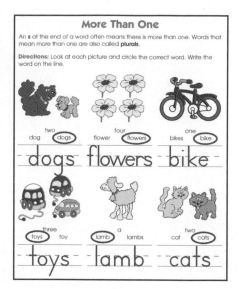

two dog (dogs) — dogs

four flower (flowers) — flowers

one bikes (bike) — bike

three (toys) toy — toys

a (lamb) lambs — lamb

two cat (cats) — cats

226

One Is Not Enough!

A plural noun means more than one. To make nouns that end in **x**, **s**, **ss**, **sh**, or **ch** plural, add **es**.

Example: Barry filled one **box** with sand.
Barry filled four **boxes** with sand.

Directions: Write the plural form of each noun below.

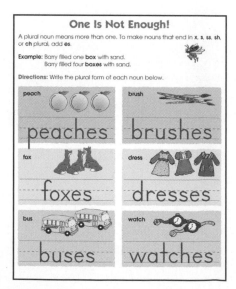

peach — peaches

brush — brushes

fox — foxes

dress — dresses

bus — buses

watch — watches

227

Use the Clues

Directions: Write each word from the word box in the correct place. Remember that plural forms usually end in **s**.

| kites | star | chick | foxes | matches | lunch |

One

star
chick   lunch

More Than One (Plural)

kites
matches
foxes

228

Sentences That Tell

Some sentences tell something. Every **telling sentence** ends with a **period**.

Example: The bird sings.

Directions: Circle only the sentences that tell something.

1. (Two turtles sat on a log.)
2. (One turtle fell off.)
3. Did you see her?
4. (She swam away.)
5. (The water is cold.)
6. Can you swim?

229

Sentences

Sentences begin with capital letters.

Directions: Read the sentences and write them below. Begin each sentence with a capital letter.

Example: the cat is fat.

The cat is fat.

my dog is big.

My dog is big.

the boy is sad.

The boy is sad.

bikes are fun!

Bikes are fun!

dad can bake.

Dad can bake.

230

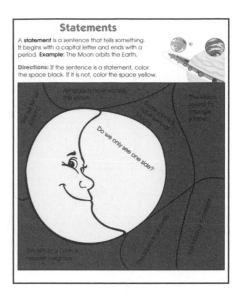

Statements

A **statement** is a sentence that tells something. It begins with a capital letter and ends with a period. **Example:** The Moon orbits the Earth.

Directions: If the sentence is a statement, color the space black. If it is not, color the space yellow.

Do we only see one side?

231

Writing Sentences

A **sentence** begins with a capital letter and ends with a period.

Directions: Read the two sentences on each line. Draw a line between the two sentences. Then, write each sentence correctly.

i have a new bike —— it is red

I have a new bike.

It is red.

we are twins —— we look just alike

We are twins.

We look just alike.

the baby is crying —— she wants a bottle

The baby is crying.

She wants a bottle.

232

Making Sentences

A **sentence** tells a whole idea.

Directions: Cut out and glue each picture and group of words together to make a sentence.

Six candles	are on the cake.
The rabbit	has four carrots.
The apple	is on a dish.
A little spider	makes a web.

233

Sentence Building

Sentences can tell a story.

Directions: Read each sentence. Cut out and glue the sentence that tells what happened next. Write a sentence that tells what could happen after that.

Mary went to bed and quickly fell asleep.
> She began to have an amazing dream.

Brad saw something shiny in the grass.
> He bent down to see what it was.

Sally wanted a pet for her birthday.
> Her mom took her to the pet store.

235

Completing Sentences

A **sentence** must make sense.

Directions: Match each sentence with an ending which makes sense. Circle the correct ending.

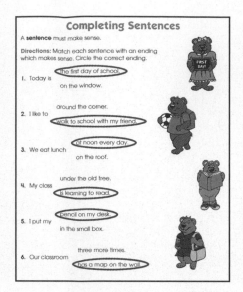

1. Today is
   - (the first day of school.)
   - on the window.

2. I like to
   - around the corner.
   - (walk to school with my friend.)

3. We eat lunch
   - (at noon every day.)
   - on the roof.

4. My class
   - under the old tree.
   - (is learning to read.)

5. I put my
   - (pencil on my desk.)
   - in the small box.

6. Our classroom
   - three more times.
   - (has a map on the wall.)

237

Subjects of Sentences

The **subject** of a sentence tells who or what does something.

Examples: Polar bears love cold weather.
The bear's coat is thick.

Directions: Circle the subject of each sentence.

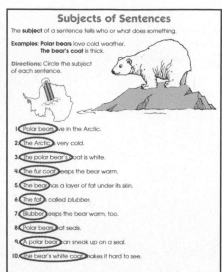

1. (Polar bears) live in the Arctic.
2. (The Arctic) is very cold.
3. (The polar bear's coat) is white.
4. (The fur coat) keeps the bear warm.
5. (The bear) has a layer of fat under its skin.
6. (The fat) is called *blubber*.
7. (Blubber) keeps the bear warm, too.
8. (Polar bears) eat seals.
9. (A polar bear) can sneak up on a seal.
10. (The bear's white coat) makes it hard to see.

238

Predicates of Sentences

The **predicate** of a sentence tells what the subject is or does.

Examples: Parrots **are not all alike**.
Some parrots **can learn tricks**.

Directions: Circle the predicate of each sentence.

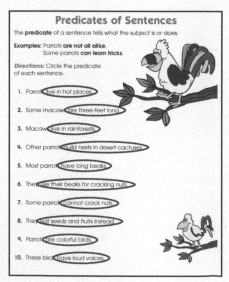

1. Parrots (live in hot places.)
2. Some macaws (are three-feet long.)
3. Macaws (live in rainforests.)
4. Other parrots (build nests in desert cactuses.)
5. Most parrots (have long beaks.)
6. They (use their beaks for cracking nuts.)
7. Some parrots (cannot crack nuts.)
8. They (eat seeds and fruits instead.)
9. Parrots (are colorful birds.)
10. These birds (have loud voices.)

239

Questions

A **question** is a sentence that asks something. It begins with a capital letter and ends with a question mark.

Example: Have you ever visited a farm? What animals lived on the farm?

Directions: If the sentence is a question, put a **question mark** at the end and color the barn red. If it is not, draw an **X** on the barn.

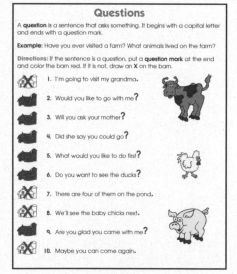

1. I'm going to visit my grandma.
2. Would you like to go with me?
3. Will you ask your mother?
4. Did she say you could go?
5. What would you like to do first?
6. Do you want to see the ducks?
7. There are four of them on the pond.
8. We'll see the baby chicks next.
9. Are you glad you came with me?
10. Maybe you can come again.

240

More Questions

Directions: A **question** begins with a capital letter and ends with a question mark. Look at each picture of Panda. Ask Panda a question to go with each picture.

Sample questions:

Is it Panda's birthday?

What kind of cookies did he bake?

What is the name of the book?

Did Panda make a snowman?

241

Changing Sentences

The order of words can change a sentence.

Directions: Read each telling sentence. Change the order of the words to make an asking sentence. **Example:**

The clown is happy.
Is the clown happy?

The boy can swim.
Can the boy swim?

The bell will ring.
Will the bell ring?

The popcorn is hot.
Is the popcorn hot?

The flowers are lovely.
Are the flowers lovely?

242

Sentences That Ask

Some sentences ask something. An **asking sentence** is called a **question**. A question ends with a **question mark**.

Example: What is your name?

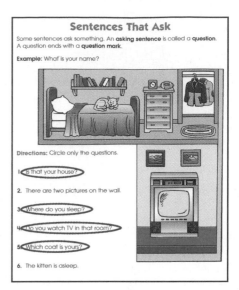

Directions: Circle only the questions.

1. (Is that your house?)
2. There are two pictures on the wall.
3. (Where do you sleep?)
4. (Do you watch TV in that room?)
5. (Which coat is yours?)
6. The kitten is asleep.

243

Questions, Questions

A **question** begins with a capital letter and ends with a question mark.

Directions: Write each question correctly on the line.

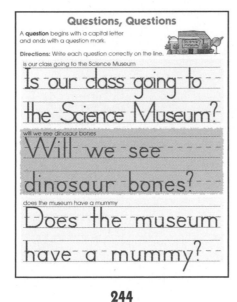

is our class going to the Science Museum
Is our class going to the Science Museum?

will we see dinosaur bones
Will we see dinosaur bones?

does the museum have a mummy
Does the museum have a mummy?

244

I'm So Excited!

The end mark **!** shows that you are excited. Use it to end a sentence that shows strong feelings.

Example: What a beautiful day this is!

Directions: Read these sentences. Write **?** or **!** after each sentence.

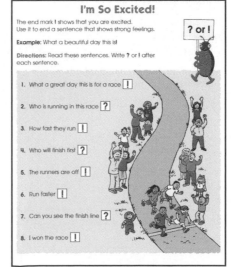

1. What a great day this is for a race !
2. Who is running in this race ?
3. How fast they run !
4. Who will finish first ?
5. The runners are off !
6. Run faster !
7. Can you see the finish line ?
8. I won the race !

245

Surprising Sequence

Some sentences show a strong feeling and end with an **exclamation mark** (!). A surprising sentence may be only one or two words showing fear, surprise, or pain, such as "Oh, no!"

Directions: Put a **period** at the end of the sentences that tell something. Put an **exclamation mark** at the end of the sentences that show a strong feeling. Put a **question mark** at the end of the sentences that ask a question.

1. The cheetah can run very fast.

2. Wow!

3. Look at that cheetah go!

4. Can you run fast?

5. Oh, my!

6. You're faster than I am.

7. Let's run together.

8. We can run as fast as a cheetah.

9. What fun!

10. Do you think cheetahs get tired?

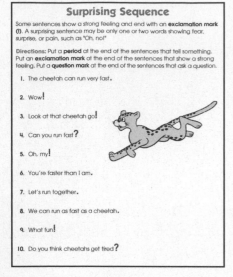

246

Sentence Sequence

The words in a sentence must be in the correct order.

Directions: Cut out and glue the words in the correct order to tell about each picture.

1.

| My family | is going | to the beach. |

2.

| We are taking | a basket | of food. |

3.

| It's fun | to swim | in the ocean. |

247

Word Order

Word order is the order of words in a sentence which makes sense.

Directions: Cut out the words and put them in the correct order. Glue each sentence on another sheet of paper.

| I | like | to | ride | my | bike. |

| It | is | hot | and | sunny. |

| I | can | drink | water. |

| My | mom | plays | with | me. |

| The | dog | do | can | tricks. |

| Can | you | go | to | the | store? |

249

ABC Order

Sometimes, words are put in **ABC order**. That means that if a word starts with **a**, it comes first. If it starts with **b**, it comes next, and so on in the order of the alphabet.

Directions: Circle the first letter of each word below. Then, put the words in ABC order. The first one is done for you.

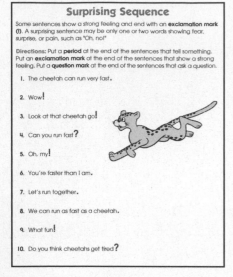

ⓒar ⓑird ⓜoon ⓣwo ⓝest ⓕan

bird

car

moon

two

fan

nest

ⓒard ⓓog ⓟig ⓑike ⓢun ⓟie

card

dog

bike

pig

pie

sun

251

ABC Order

Directions: Put each row of words in ABC order. If the first letters of two words are the same, look at the second or third letters.

Example:

1. __1__ candy __2__ carrot __4__ duck __3__ dance

2. __2__ cold __4__ hot __1__ carry __3__ hit

3. __2__ flash __1__ fan __3__ fun __4__ garden

4. __2__ seat __4__ sun __1__ saw __3__ sit

5. __3__ row __1__ ring __2__ rock __4__ run

6. __2__ truck __3__ turn __4__ twin __1__ talk

7. __1__ seven __2__ shoe __4__ soap __3__ smell

8. __1__ pay __2__ penny __4__ pocket __3__ plant

252

Make your own book called "Introducing..." with the cardboard pages attached to the back of this workbook. Have fun drawing and coloring the pictures!

Skunks live in the forest.

Fish live in the sea.

I live in a _____

with my family.

8

Introducing . . . .

_____

Born on _____

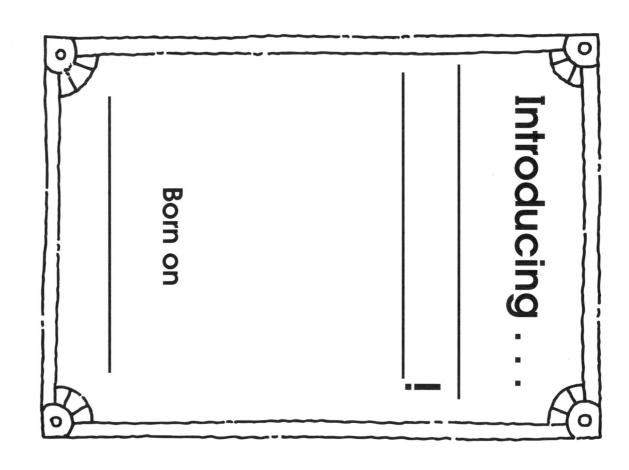

1

I wear _____ in _____ weather.

A bear eats berries.

A shark eats fish.

6

A dog has fur.

A bird has feathers.

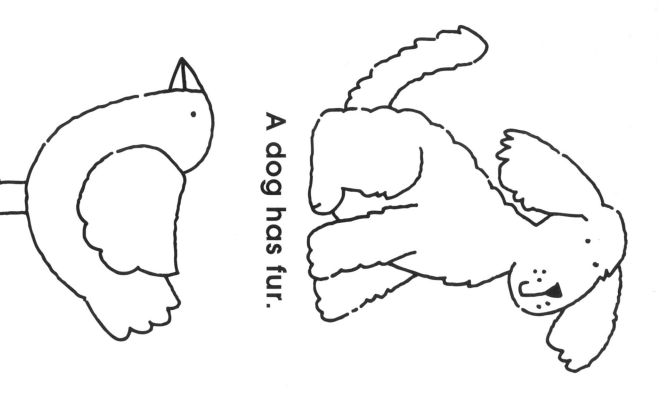

I eat _____ with

my favorite dish.

3

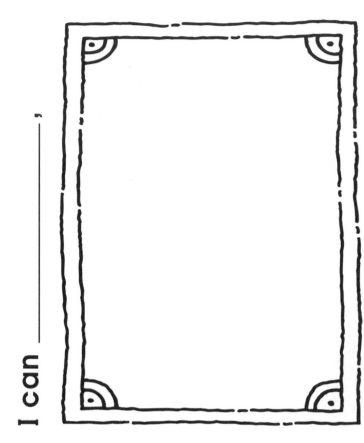

I can _____,

and I can _____.

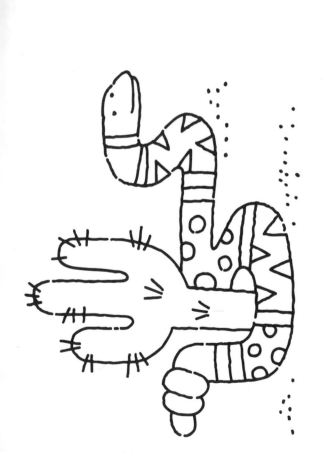

Snakes can slither.

Rabbits can hop.